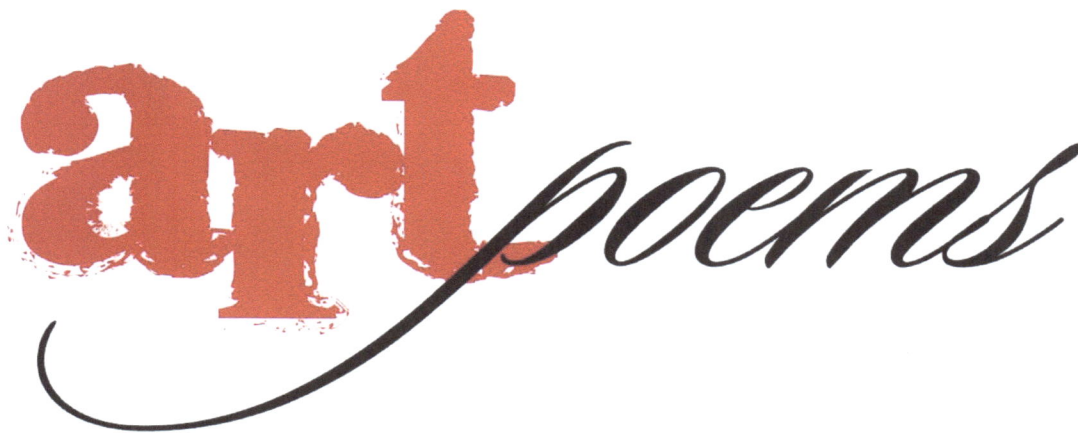

2017
Art and Poems
In Collaboration

Lorraine Walker Williams, Chair

Joseph Pacheco, Vice Chair

Larry Stiles, Secretary-Treasurer

Beth Everhart, Book Design

ArtPoems, Inc.
www.artpoems.org

Aquila, divine

Inspired by Maria Bouloux's "Wistful Glance"

Like the two pinnacles of a westwork piercing the grey sky,
     The gleam of the potentate of Nyx, of misplaced motherhood
—A blacksmith in birthright: her eyes the hammer, the fire, the stone
     A burnished, branding stare, a predator through roseate glass, a kiss through glassine.

She's a mess of didactic peckings from catechism and eschatology
     And cosmo and a scorpionic stellium dripping with illicit sovereignty,
Dripping with liquid onyx, slipping from her jaw, down from her eyes,
     Bleeding from her scalp, spilling onto her coxal.

But she dreams of sweeping the mountains aside
     Skimming the oldest water with her fingers and licking off the salt,
Finding herself in tartarus just to chance a look at her daughter,
     But she finds she's always searching in her wake, her eyes twisted behind.

- Marissa Douglass

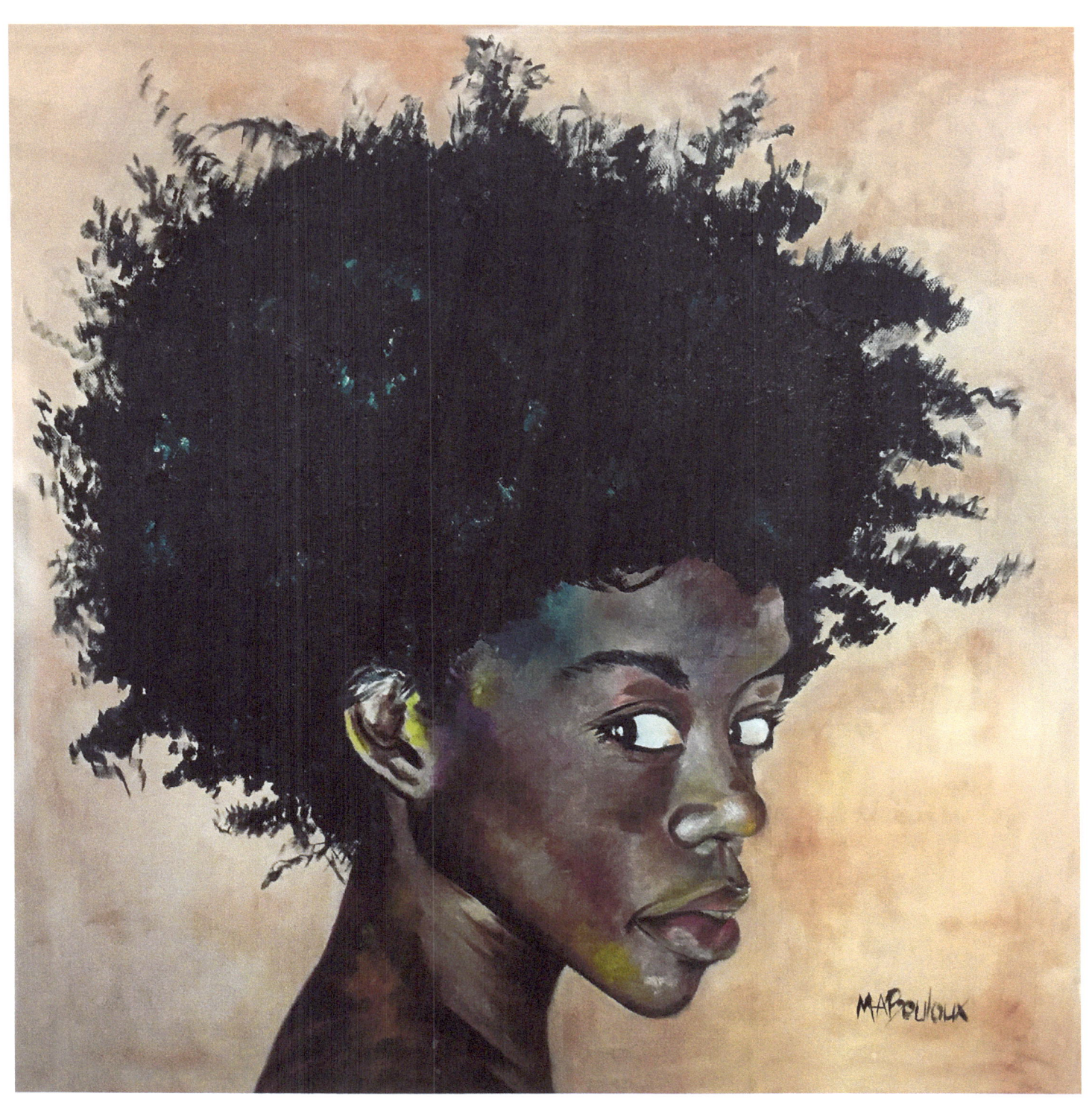

Wistful Glance—*Maria Bouloux*

The Born

Inspiration for Linda Lally's "Tiger Mother"

I waited in the
cloverweeds
to see there the brahman child,
to see he who permeates the veil,
he who is not aware of his male-ness,
he who all at once is a tiger and an infant,
once suckling at the dark blue breasts of *his* mother,
the fair pink nipples of Titania,
the pale orange belly of a tigress,
drinking the milk and honey and
mineral clear liquid of this earth,
lapping the dazzling liquor of breath and pulse,
drinking straight from the earth like a jug,
licking like the planet is a lollipop,
like the planet is satiating to
him, who was once like amber inside a virgin, to
him, who as a blue skinned changeling is mothered by earth,
and gravel, and typhoon, to
him whose love is fostered by a tiger mother whose
play is lonesomely subsonic, to
him, suspended in fairie bower,
cooed and prickled by the genderless voices,
a fountain of mouthed soundlessness, to
him, who dances a violent army of fiddles and pipe flutes
and hollow howling, to
him who chants in secret prayers
and asks for infinity to find him, him
who has no mother, a mother.

- Marissa Douglass

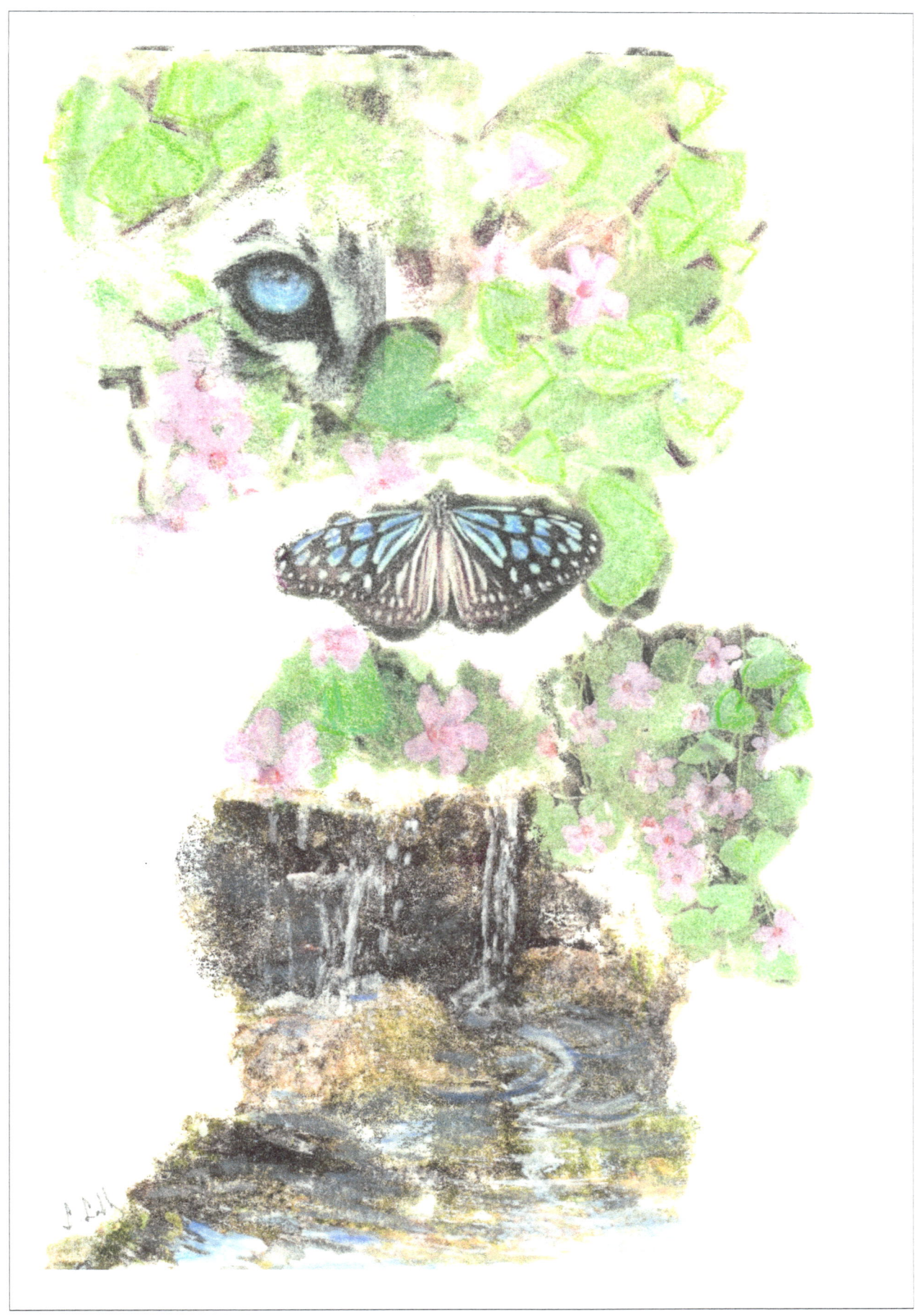

Tiger Mother—*Linda Lally*

Sanctuary

Inspired by Dennis Church's "Naples, Florida 2010 (from Public Attire series)"

She tells the kids Pink Panther is here to zap cancer
whistles and sashays the bald girl's wheelchair
swings a la "Country Time Barn Dance" her nurses
who call her "Boss Lady"
Sings goofy songs as she finds a tiny vein
Cracks corny jokes as she threads a catheter
Tells a boy as much truth as he can bear about his first chemo session
Gathers broken pieces of the sobbing Mom, swaddles her
No chaplains at this ungodly hour

She trudges to the old Toyota two hours after sunrise
Last thing she wants is back on her feet, forced to talk
to one more, single human being
But, the market's siren call is obliged to be obeyed

Air cleans the glaze of "nurses' station buffet" from her palette
Out of tune fiddles rinse beeping monitors, shouted codes, phones
driven to leave messages, even as the normal world sleeps
Sunshine scours sinuses of almighty disinfectants, overlay waft of fear
some from tiny patients, more from parents, and secreted behind eyes
of their caretakers

Loosening senses, unbuckling her Id's restraints just like her Mom's ecstasy
peeling herself from her girdle after Mass
Bags fill with overpriced honey, handfuls of tomatoes and green beans, apricot bars
Mennonite girls talked her into, reminding herself go back
for that bunch of flowers (I never treat myself)
Photos of father and son showing off treasures gathered that day
Decade old red paint glistens, fresh scent of paste wax
staving off ravages of sun and streets

Boss Lady soon enough, to be in fresh scrubs (maybe Scooby Doo tomorrow?)
departing sanctuary when lucid folks ready for supper
back to the kids and drowsy, harried parents on Three West, but for now
she dreams of saving crisp green beans Mañana, allowing just one
gooey apricot bar
to swaddle her soul

   - Dan Reed England

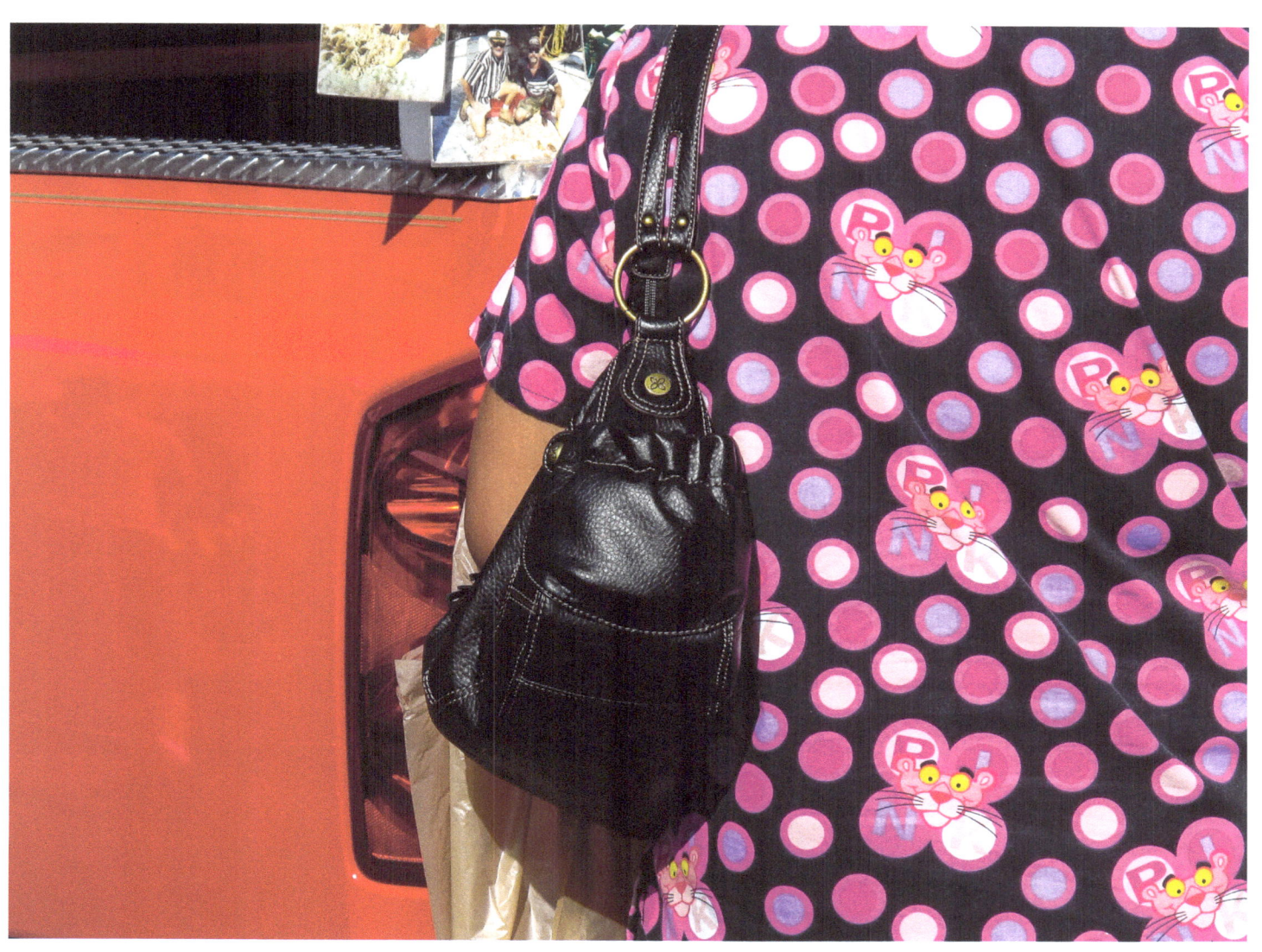

Naples Florida 2010 (from Public Attire series)—Dennis Church

Drift
Inspiration for Honey Costa's "Rainbow Memories"

I memorized that beach day with Mommy
Sand, sand, the everywhere sand
to crunch under toes
fill metal pails
sift through fingers, drift
into ocean breezes

Mommy laughed when the swoop
of seagull snatched my sandwich
Hugged away my terror cries
shouted oaths damning all
flying creatures foolish
enough to dare a return

Innocence soaking in sunshine health
drenched in delicious Coppertone
UV fears a generation away

I announced each passing
of the Piper Super Cub
towing the back and forth banner
as Mommy read out loud
over and over
"All You Can Eat 45 Foot Salad Bar Buffet"

Couples necked under beach blankets
not seeing
plane, waves, gulls, wind, sand
Mommy watched them smooching
I saw her look to a place
far away where Daddy
smooched with another lady and I
began to forget the smell
of Lucky Tiger hair tonic and scratch
of whiskers kissing
my forehead good night
I memorized that beach day with Mommy

Dan Reed England

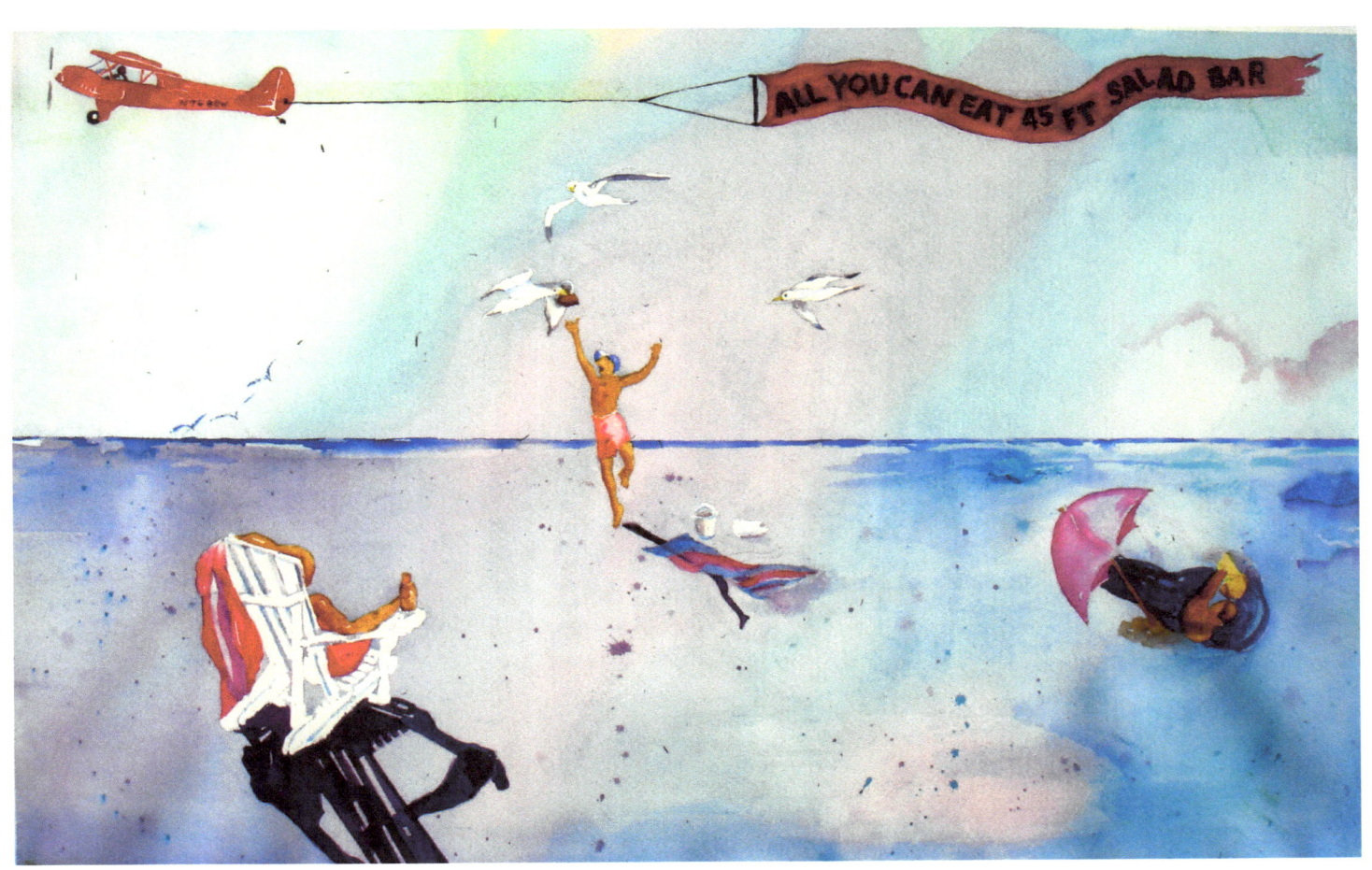

Rainbow Memories—*Honey Costa*

Klimt's Muse
Inspired by Honey Costa's "Klimt's Garden"

She is barely visible,
a specter in the field
of scarlet poppies
intoxicated by their odorless scent.
Seed after seed, she escapes,
weightless as she drifts
from dream to dream. In one
she is Klimt's muse,
a nymph wrapped in embrace,
waiting for the memorable kiss.
In another she becomes a poppy,
afire in the sun-struck field,
and she springs up in flower
after flower multiplying
in the landscape. Here in this garden
of heavenly descent, she does not cry
for rescue. But closes her eyes
and waits for the evening's
blanket of stillness.

- Joyce Berrian Ferrari

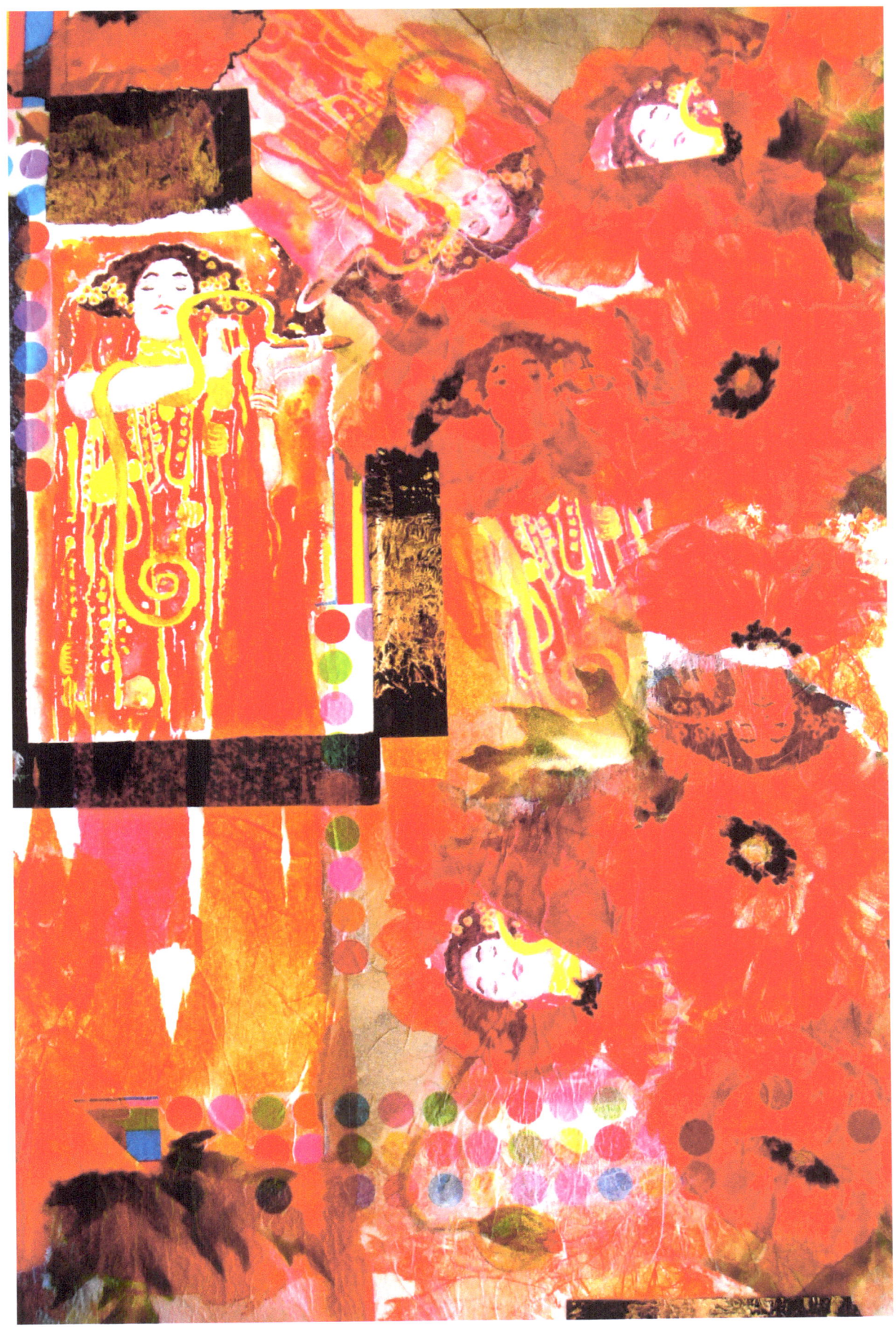

Klimt's Garden—*Honey Costa*

Almost Vanished

Inspiration for Eleanor Dominek's "Through Cypress Glades"

The distant hum
grows to a roar
an airboat crashes
   through the grassland
swamp buggies plow
   across cypress forests
the gladesman camouflaged
whiskered face
tobacco stained teeth
forages in a changing world
he keeps remnants of the old
   hunts
   fishes
   weaves tales
he loves his miserable hard life
a florida cajun sequestered
in the neighborhood of contradictions
   lawless honorable
   wasteful hardworking
   ascetic indulgent
marshy glades his sanctuary
of tranquility and dangers
he listens and watches
whip-poor-will and warbler
alligators amongst sawgrass
deceptive manchineel trees
pious cypress
   limbs outstretched
carnivorous bladder plant
   erect above still waters
   traps creatures below
cowhorn orchid thrives
   amidst poison wood

tonight the gladesman returns
at dusk he sits at his table
   grits and gravy served
   by his bony wife
tonight he sleeps and dreams
the ghosts of Okeechobee
echo the stories
of ancient gladesmen
of the almost vanished
Mescosukee and Seminole
   specters who live
   deep in the primeval forest
listen carefully to detect
the rumble of rickety oxcarts
a hooting barred owl
chanting tribal rhythms
lull the sleepy swampland
bojangles lifts his heels
   dances to an ancestral ballad
red-haired smelly skunkape
rambles on big feet
   wary of invaders in ochopee
the ghost ship waits
to return the gladesman
back to his place of honor
and glory

Joyce Berrian Ferrari

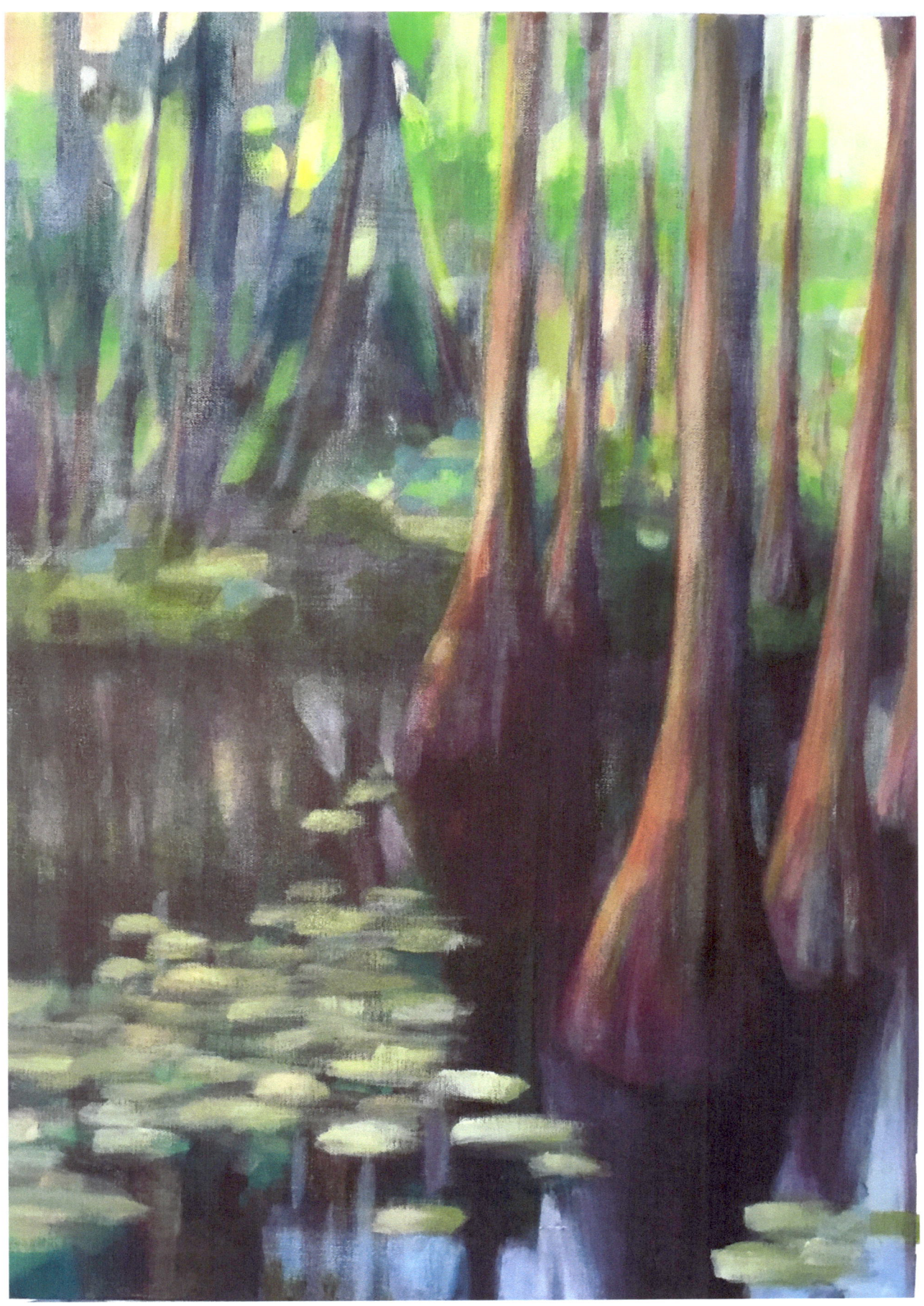

Through Cypress Glades—*Eleanor Dominek*

An Artist's Journey

Inspired by Berry van Boekel's "Volendam"

One of us here—
child of Volendam—
will leave behind
wooden shoes,
bonneted head dress—
the stuff of homeland,
custom and comfort

One of us, tugged by
tinctures of turpentine
and sun-splashed oils,
will push through
this postcard pose,
seeking the promise
of other shores

but will find
in Antwerp and Lake Erie
icicles too frigid,
a chill too constraining
for canvas creations.

Then one of us—a child now—
will slip onto sandy soil,
laugh delightedly as
paint brushes awaken.

And, yes,
one of us here

will fuse forever,
the fronds and shoes,
the skirts and bonnets
into a new

being,

breath

and

belonging.

- Chris Godwin

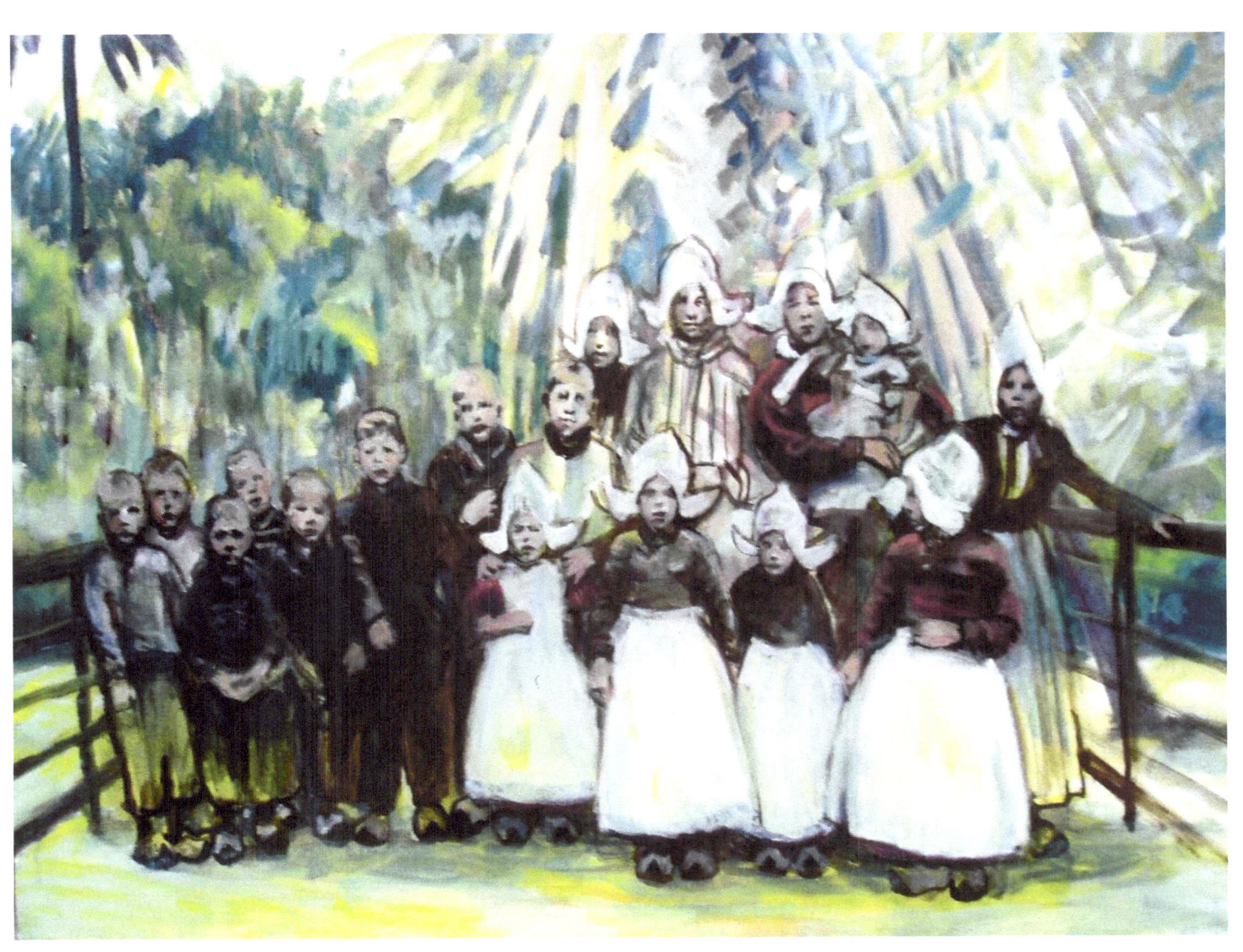

Volendam—Berry van Boekel

Museum: After Hour

Inspiration for Beth Everhart's "Athena Awakens"

When the lights go dim
In Olympia,
The gods remember
They are human.

Apollo lowers his sculpted arm
Uncurls sensuously curved fingers
Leans lithe but lazy.

Athena, after a full day of serious intent
Championing eternal wisdom,
Sighs relief, flexes forehead,
Neck, even one
Exquisitely cramped foot.

While Poseidon, dry as marble dust,
Casts for water, here, there,
Anywhere,
Even in those battered bottles
From tourist trash.

One thousand echoes—
"no flash, please!"—
Later, the Sphinx,
That weighty presence,
Actually turns his ear this way
And that
In the cool silent air.

And a hoard of satyrs, 'til now
Frozen in mid-temptation,
Slide to the polished floor
And
Dance, baby, dance.

     - Chris Godwin

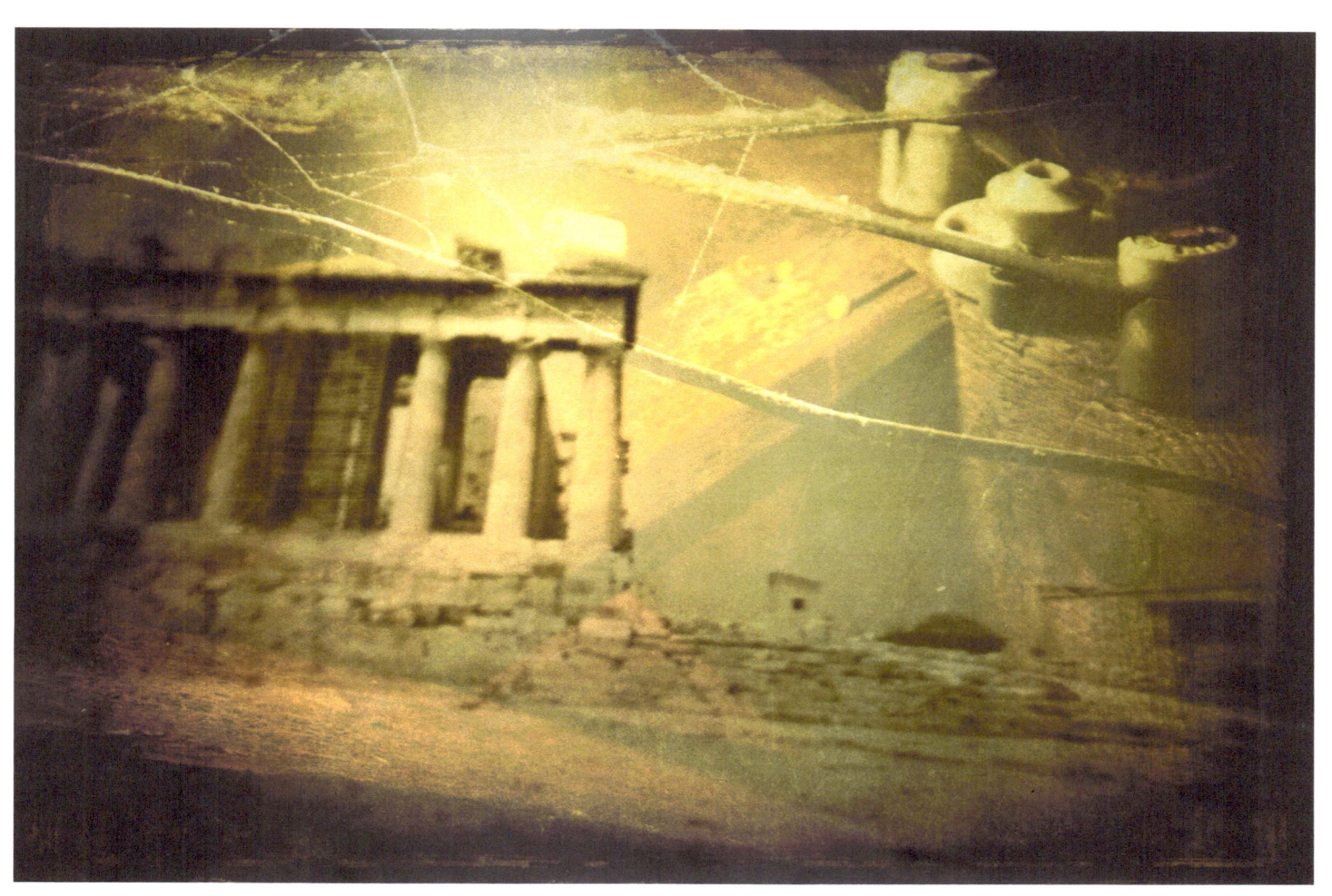

Athena Awakens—*Beth Everhart*

Divorce

Inspired by Linda Lally's painting, "Divorce"

The word slides, slippery, off her tongue
He understands once uttered,
The process has begun.
Shudders, as he envisions it unraveling, undone.
Unhappy ending for their children, still so young,
Caught in this wreckage they'll create
Where once love lived, he senses growing hate.

No longer will that slip of gossamer lace
Dangle off her shoulder like a romance to be read
No late night movies
Or languid mornings spent in bed
"Leave me now" is what she said.

He cannot comprehend his sin
Feels unjustly punished
As anger and confusion mount within.
All those words they've sung, then later flung
Circle, scrambled and competing
In his head.

He remembers when his heart caught
At just the sight or scent or thought of her.
His desire to capture what's been lost
Nearly overwhelms his need to prove she's wrong,
Has been all along
Accuses her, again, of being the Drama Queen
Compromise,
A song he never chose to sing.

Sadness settles slowly, like a fog
As his mind wanders this labyrinth of love and loss
Refusing to recognize the pattern that has caused this pain
Failing to understand
Why love will not remain.

-Sandy Greco

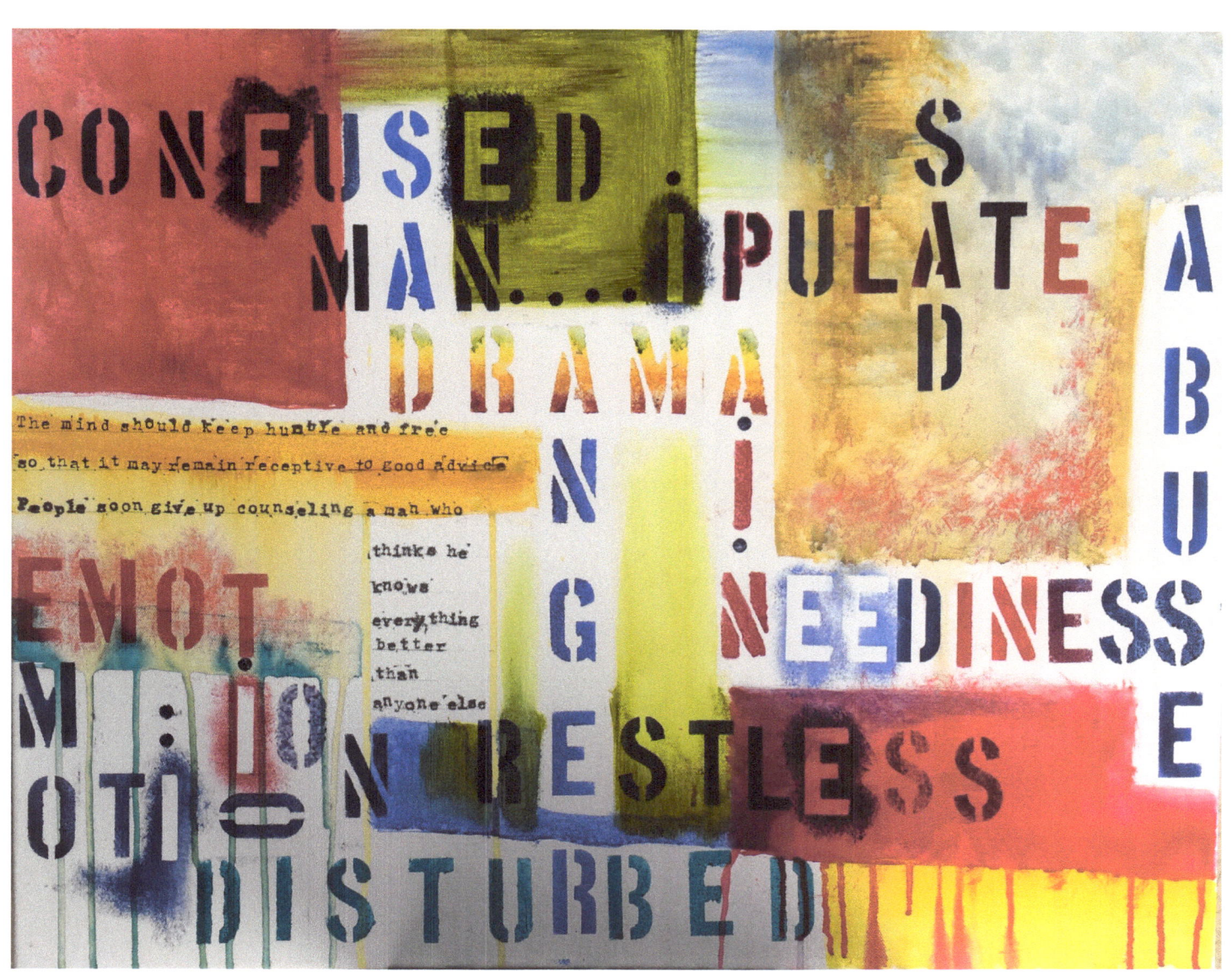

Divorce—*Linda Lally*

Ordinary Day

Inspiration for Scott Guelcher's "Ordinary Day?"

Ordinary day
In the grocery store
Rushing, deciding
Whether pears or peaches would be best
As you reach for everything in the cart,
Your little hands
Trying endlessly to pull things off the shelves.

Exasperated, I tell you to stop
Something will break, come crashing down.
Thinking, I have no time for this.
Not understanding,
This is all the time I have
And I am throwing it away.

Distracted, believing things elsewhere more important,
Not recognizing that you
Are all that ever really mattered.

It took me too long to learn
The broken pickle jar was never of any consequence
And this never was an ordinary day.

\- Sandy Greco

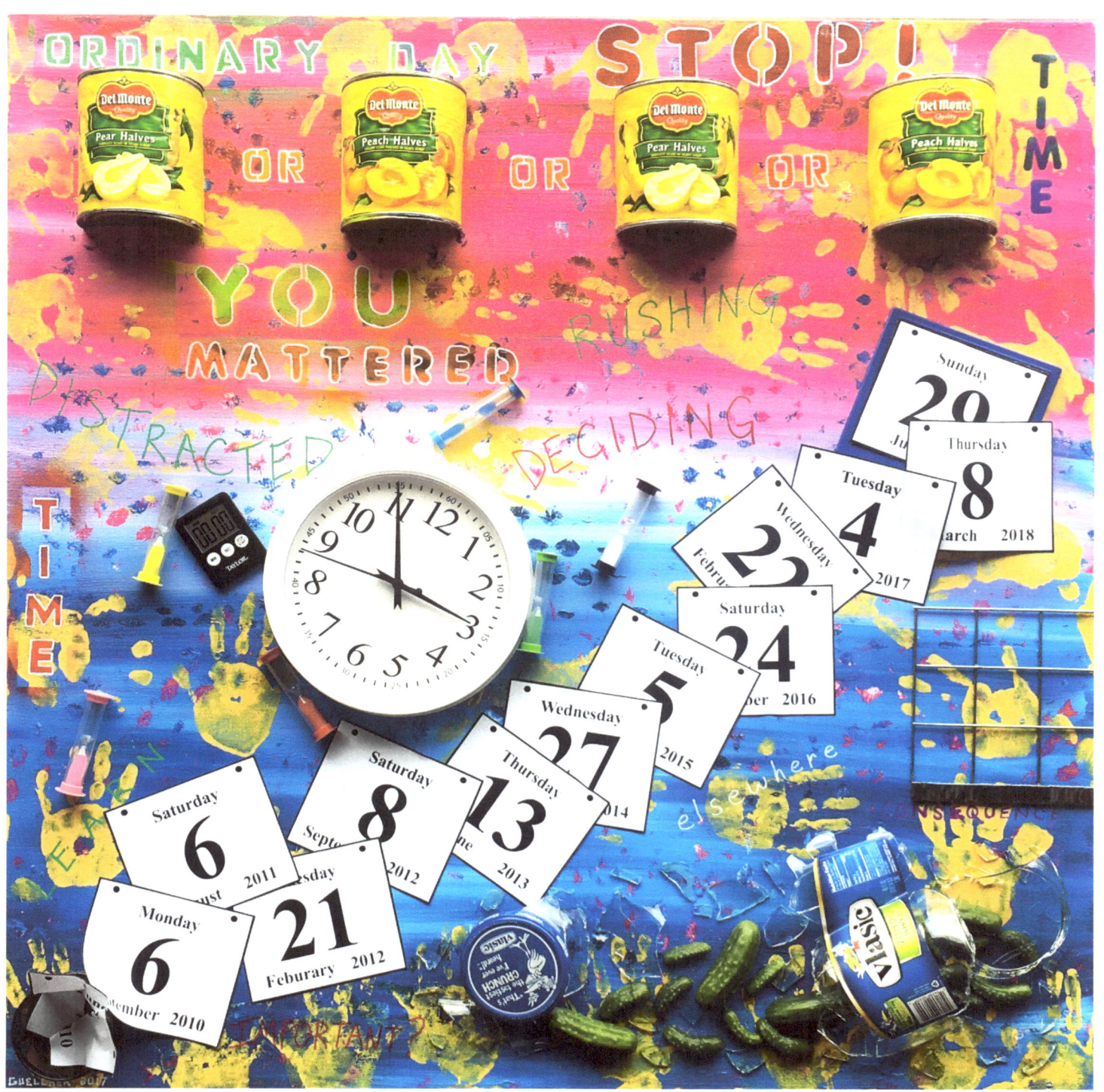

Ordinary Day? —*Scott Guelcher*

Why Does the Sky Cry?

Inspired by Roy Rodriguez' "Closed Windows"

The sky cries--see tears
stream down closed windows with bars.

Why does the sky cry? Why do I?
Why does the earth sob at conflicts, wars,
mobs who hate one another--why?

The U.S. is involved
in over 100 conflicts, the world many more.
Why do we struggle so, heads throb?

The number of people who die
often begins with 1000s, soon more,
depending on countries, tribes, cultures,

and the issues over which they fight.
Poets live inside metaphor
which can stand fast yet offer others,

may be mundane *and* mysterious.
Metaphor is found in image
and suggestive complexity,

enriched narrative, and we
understand that imagination
transforms the literal,

frees us from tyranny
of that often repeated line:
But that's how it happened.

Picasso said it can teach us
that art may lie to tell the truth.

        - Mary Beth Lundgren

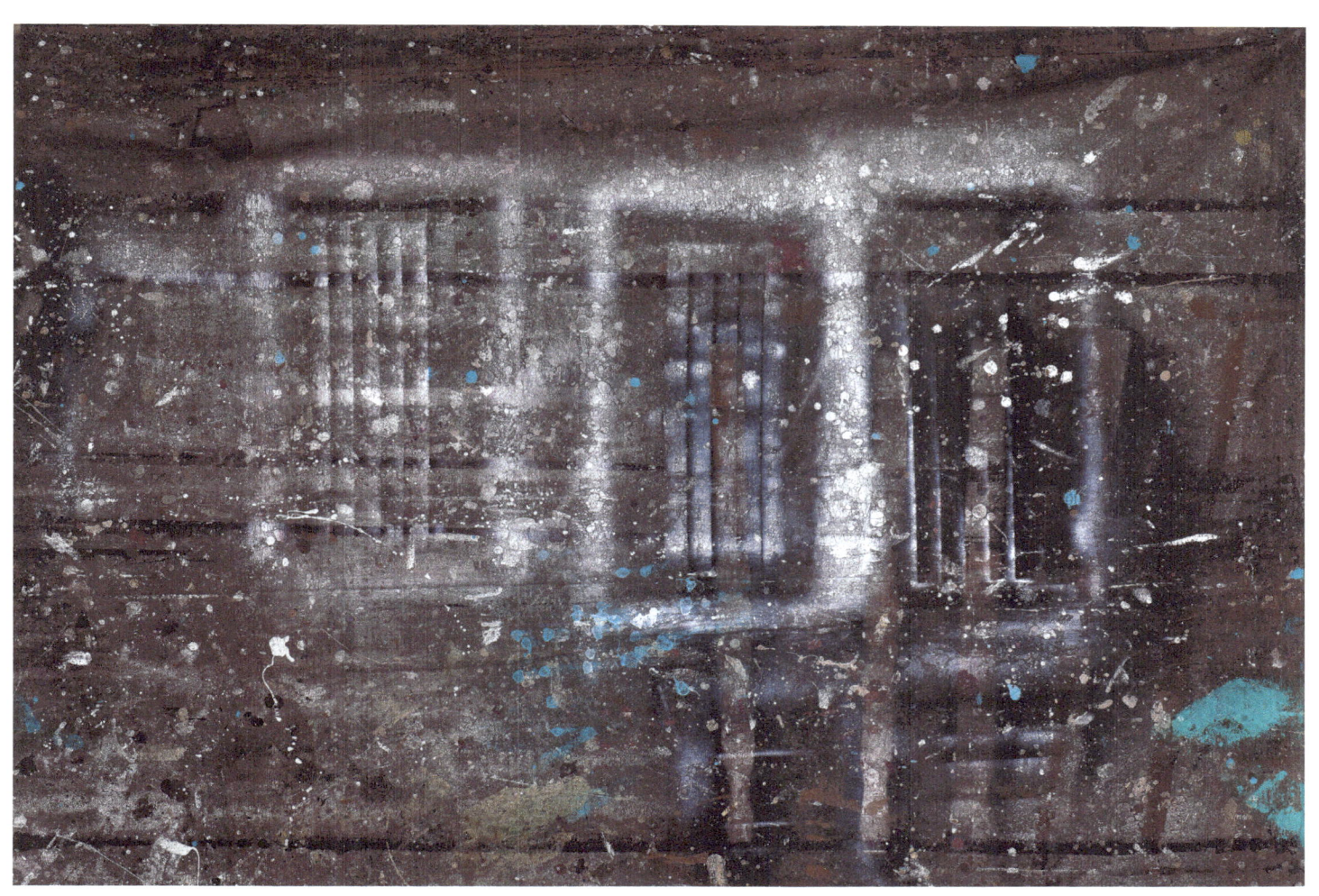

Closed Windows—*Roy Rodriguez*

In Our Garden

Inspiration for Paul David Adamick's "In Our Garden"

Our native plant garden hums with moths, birds,
bees, dragonflies that create excitement
from pink powderpuff trees canopied overhead
to sweet mimosa, carpet beneath our feet.

Blue spiderwort blooms clear as a baby's eyes
but only mornings when it grows in shade;
afternoons blossoms fold themselves
as hands do in prayer, turn green, or drop.

White blossoms--plumbago, lantana, viburnum--
pure as newborn souls fill us with sweet scent,
light the night, bring moon's shine
as in a mirror or crystal flute.

Red, love of hummers and numbers of butterflies
makes cats wild; no matter where red firebush
and honeysuckle bloom, they seduce baby tigers.

Shadows flicker through Bahama cassia.
Tiny gold petals drift on air, echoes of coins in water
undersea. Pieces of eight, sunflowers sprawl.

Invasive, non-natives grow like spiteful children,
push in wherever, cause harm to pools, roofs.

Natives planted where happy, dance. Contrapuntal
leaf texture--shiny wild coffee, velvety necklace pod,
sharp grasses and any art--film, paint, dance--
may be a fugue. We didn't build our life to be better
than others but to be better than we used to be.

- Mary Beth Lundgren

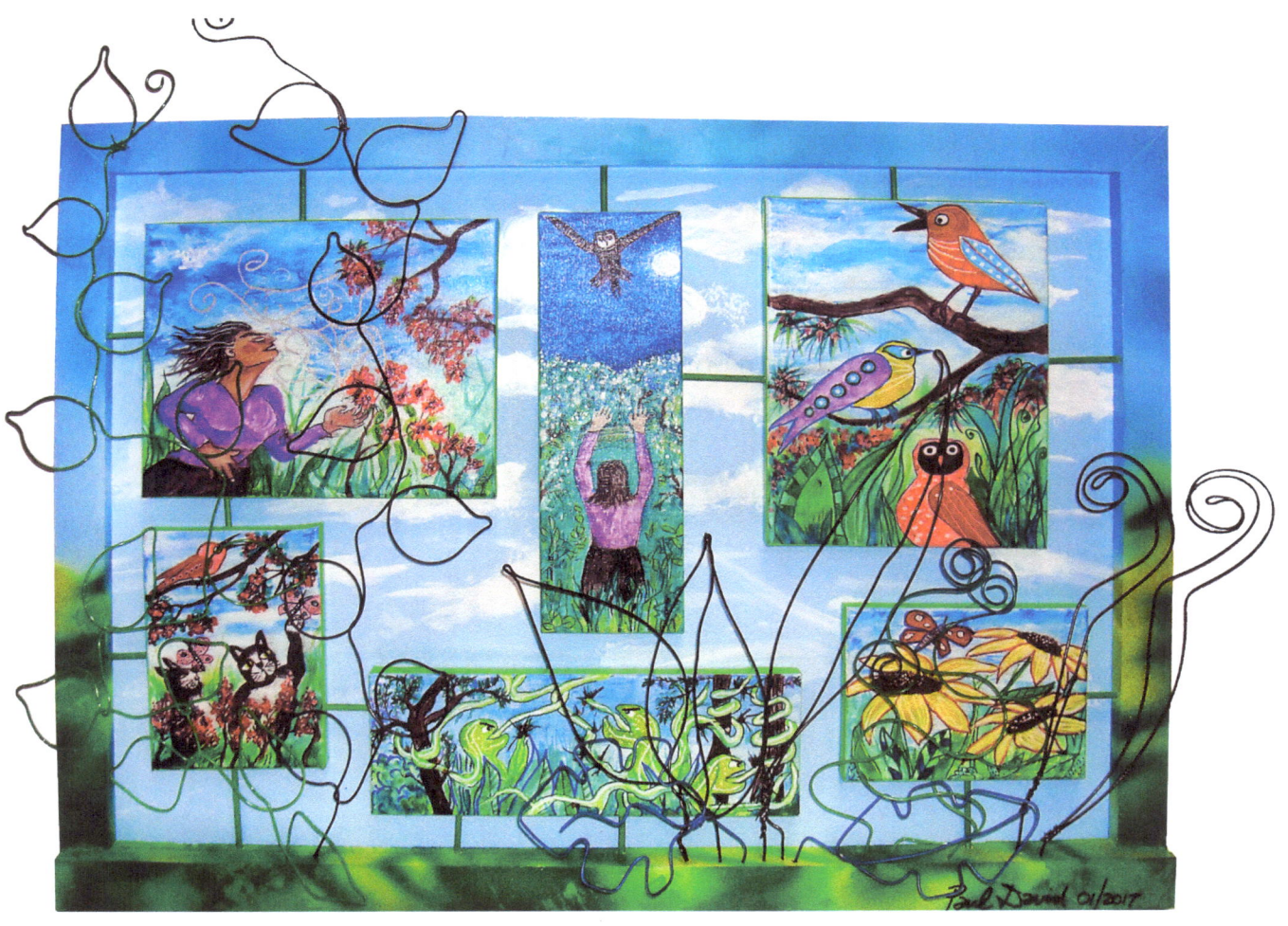

In Our Garden—*Paul David Adamick*

Bury the Garmin

Inspired by Eleanor Dominek's "Near Day's End: The Apache Trail"

One step, two steps, five hundred-two miles,
a roadmap of footprints without satellite guidance.
A trail of tears, sweat, scorched scenarios,
only an Apache can recount its oral history.

Have you pondered these round rocks,
there to tell us, here to remind us?
They did not endure one bad storm, but thousands.
Winds etched every inch, prevailing and random,
searing and solemn.

If you were privileged to sculpt with the hands of time,
would you shave off every moment with such precision?
Mark the trail, mile after mile, considering the survival of the fittest,
icons of stone, landmarks of lessons learned.

The Apache never stopped to ask for direction.
The shadows of miniature monoliths controlled their compass point.
These weathered wonders speak volumes
in full-throated tribal translation.

Have you pondered the jagged rock?
Jutting out, sharp enough to keep your distance,
far enough to marvel the magnificence,
close enough to hear words spread 'round the world.

So where are *you* headed?
Is it a long journey or weekend jaunt,
a rendezvous with a recluse,
a Twittered reunion with an old friend?

Take time to sit and listen, not one step further.
When the rains soak you to the bone,
feel the moisture fill your jaundiced joints.
Connect tribal translation with tormented tissue.

Tears, sweat, the tongues that set the trail
speak volumes when you listen with your heart.
Reach, recount, and remember a million steps,
without a Fitbit. Now kneel and bury the Garmin.

-Doug MacGregor

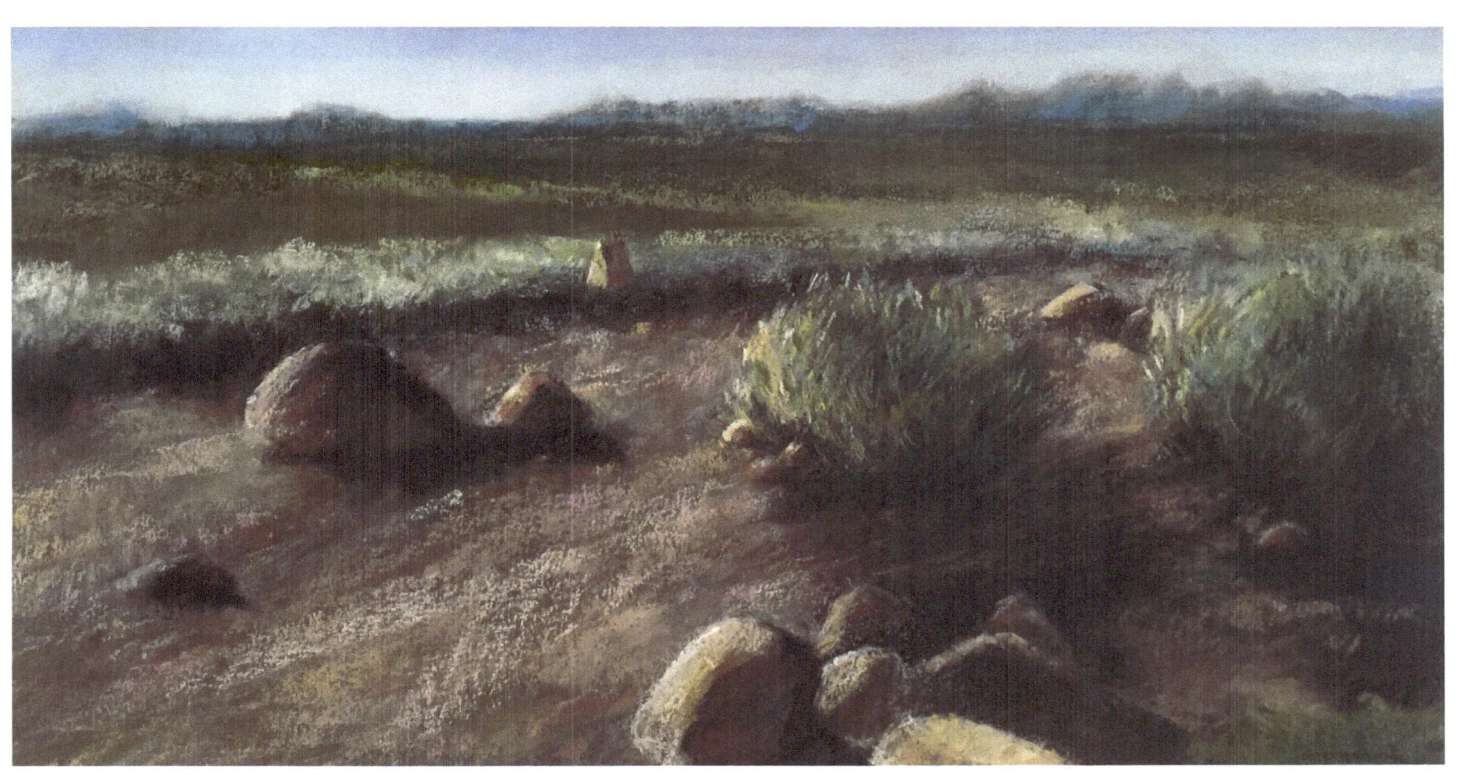

Near Day's End: The Apache Trail—*Eleanor Dominek*

Santa Has Left the Building
Inspiration for Maria Bouloux's "Packing Up"

Santa has left the building,
Many believers are still in disbelief.
The first black Santa
is leaving the People's House.

He termed out,
but left monumental marks,
not with nail holes on walls,
or solar panels on the roof.

He leaves with deeds and directives,
and countless executive privileges.
The pen is mightier than the sword;
especially Santa's pen.

Remodeling the workshop has begun.
Someone else lays claim to the
People's Deed.
Although he doesn't own it,
He will claim it as his own.

So when you remodel,
do you gut everything,
rip it to the roots,
or just paint over the walls,
with rose-colored latex?

Do you add fringes of gold-leaf,
or use rollers of electoral college red.
They may have to go over it twice,
get a second opinion, second look,
and recount the sales slip.

Our White House with a black Santa
has a moving van in the driveway.
They are carrying history out,
a Manhattan makeover is moving in.
And he is not an interior designer.

They pack away the teleprompter,
all-American jerseys with number ones,
gifts from around the world,
including a marred Nobel Prize,
a box of Cuban cigars, and a new
alphabet that includes the letters,
L-G-T-B.

Reindeer have their packing orders too.
But, don't expect them to remain grounded;
not with names like Brains,
Wonder, Patience, and Compassion;
Rigor, Resolve, Pride and Empathy.

The sled goes in last, but it doesn't fit.
They will have to get a bigger truck.
Maybe they will leave it on the front lawn as
a year-round reminder,
but, they won't.

They won't because they are too busy
in the backyard….. Already.
We can hear that pounding sound.
The defiant Donald's thud, thud, thud.

The high stakes are going in the ground.
A new white wall tower is rising,
the heights no one has ever seen.
The Superlatives are moving in.
And so goes the neighborhood.

Mrs. Claus's herb garden is all that is left.
It too will lay fallow.
Processed foods will replace organic.
Seeds of inclusion go dormant.

Santa has left the building. Yet, he did leave
some chocolate milk and
some home-made cookies to share.

-Doug MacGregor

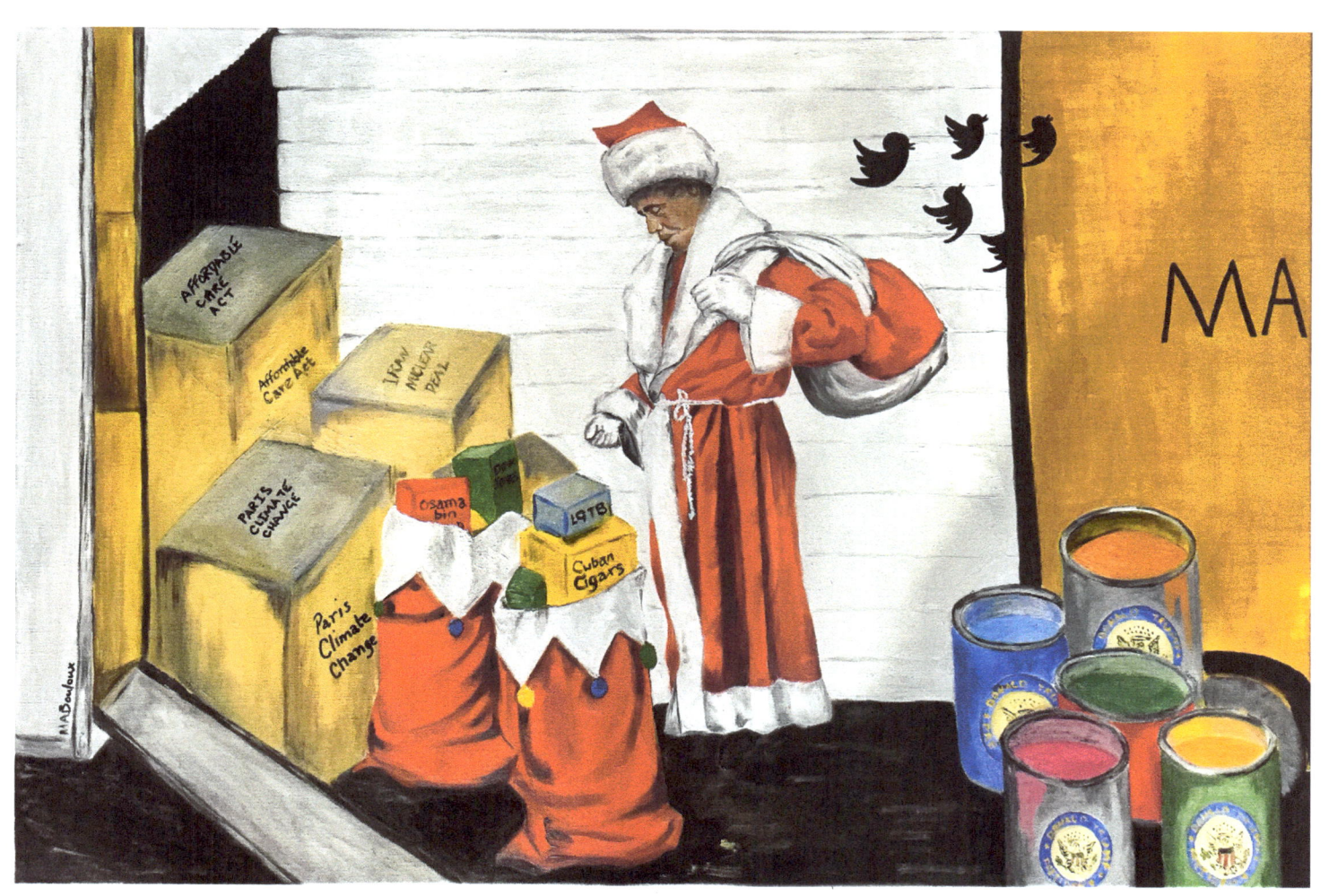

Packing Up—*Maria Bouloux*

Your Looking Glass

Inspired by Terry Lynn's "Oliver"

Yeah, I get it

You think I'm watching you watch me play in blue blossoms

A grasshopper giant of the bug species

Your wise-ass kid teasing the hue out of you

What do you think I think of you

squinting scorn

sputtering spittle

Who do you think you are, judging who you think I am

Father, I've spied into your looking glass, all the way to where

day's end ravages the light

Where flower gardens worm into compost

making soil fertile for your burial

You stand forever in a garden of cement

betrayed by your pride

This son swims through dreams of blue roses

deaf to cries blooming from the dark

-   Gary McLouth

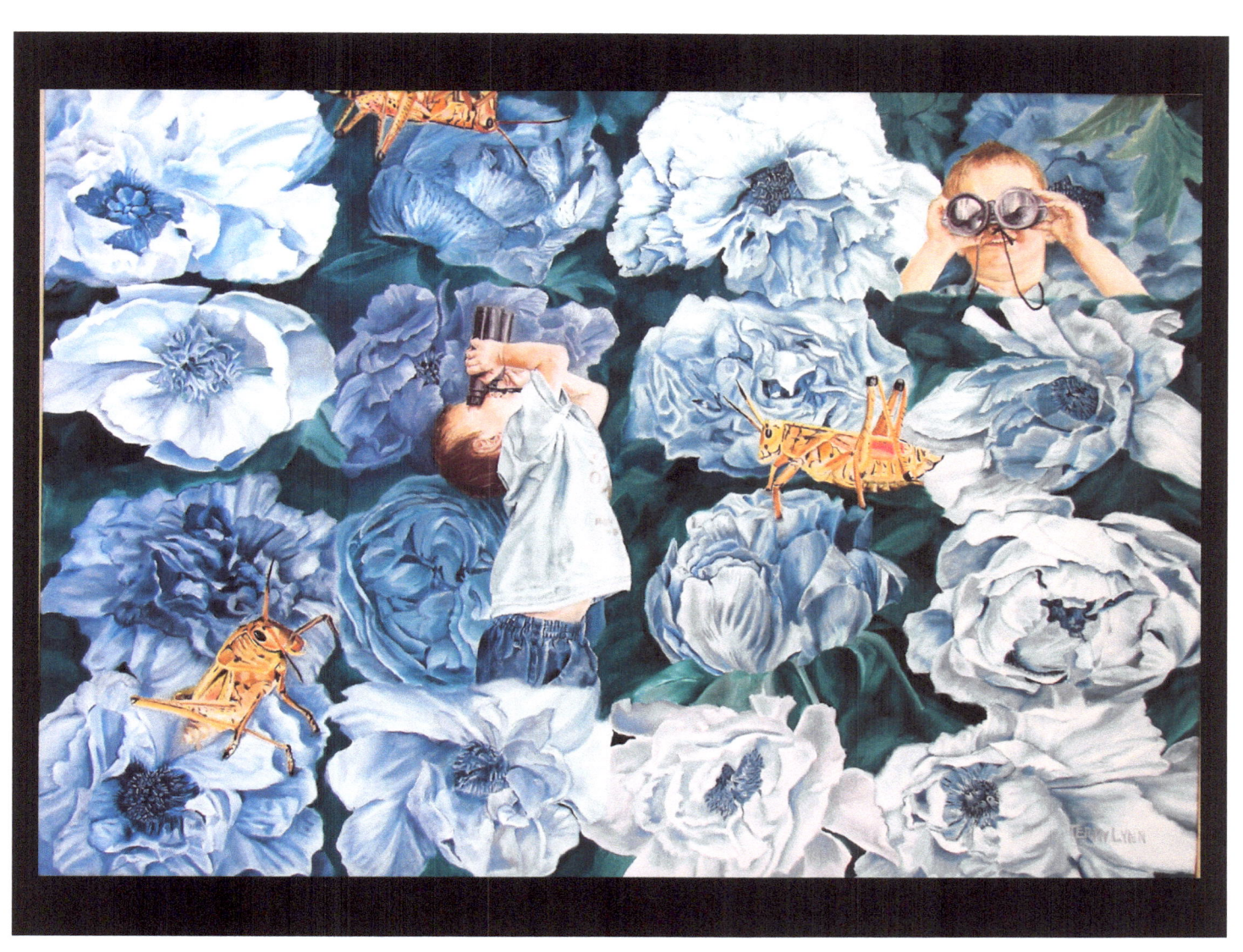

Oliver—*Terry Lynn*

Road Trip

Inspiration for Roy Rodriguez' "Trip of Memories"

Filling your shirts with wind

Was never my idea

How we would drive

East to the sea

That father and son retreat

Long shorelines, little houses

The twang of talk, muffins

Blueberry, apple, peach

It won't happen now

Who waited too long

Wandered wide of the mark

Wouldn't be right to ask

Not on this ride

The road we failed to take together.

This trip I steer alone

Your shirts strung across the back seat

Gary McLouth

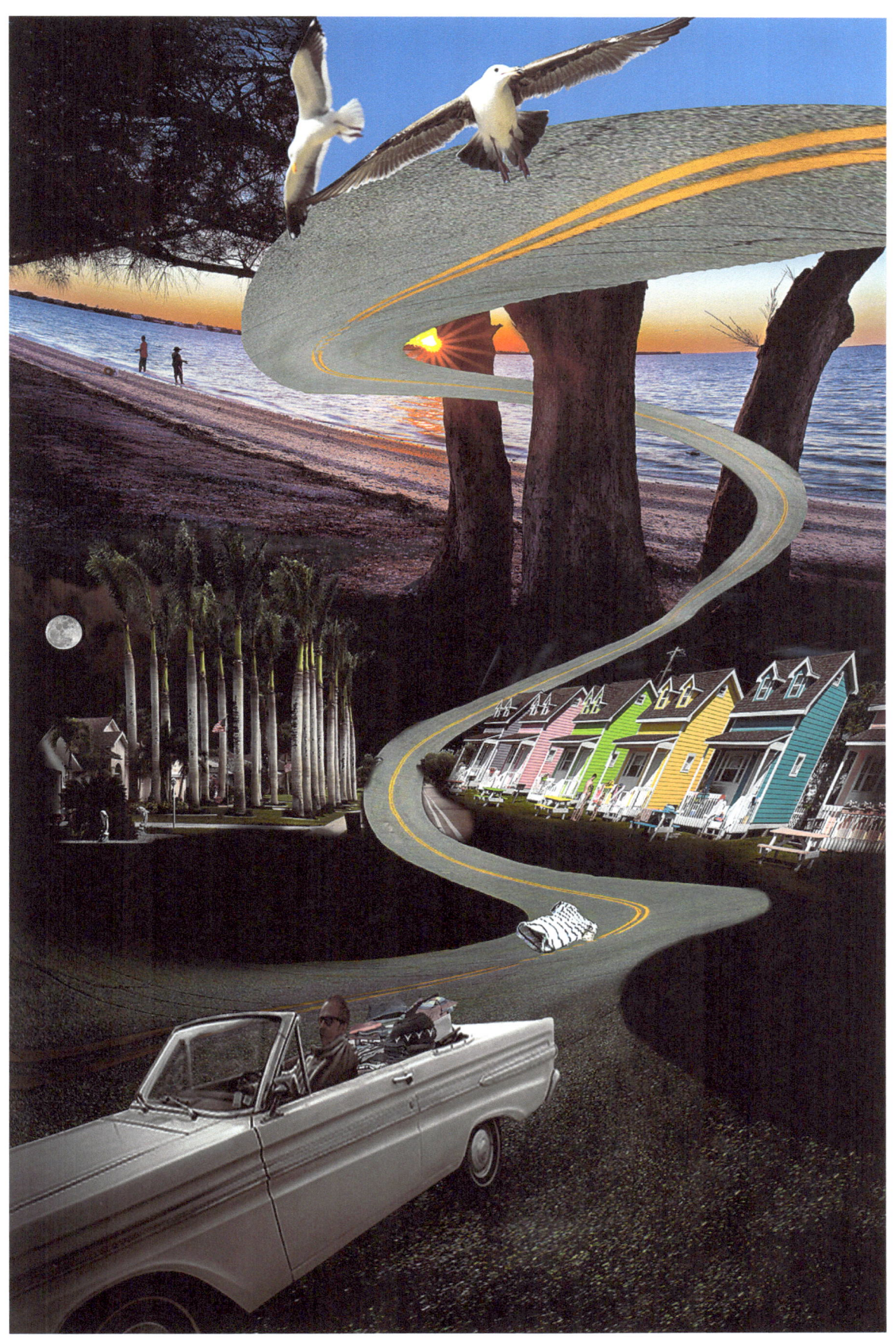

Trip of Memories—*Roy Rodriguez*

It's The Same Difference Everywhere

Inspired by Beth Everhart's "Off Prospect"

It's the same difference everywhere:
No one is ever who he wants to be,
Everyone thinks he is someone else
And anyone can do it better than he.

No one is ever who he wants to be
Till someone tells him what he wants to hear:
That anyone can do it better than he
And teach no one what he needs to know.

Now someone tells him what he wants to hear:
Don't ever listen to anyone else
Telling no one that what he needs to know
Won't hurt anyone if no one cares.

So no one listens to anyone else
Because everyone thinks he is someone else
And it doesn't hurt that no one will care:
It's the same difference everywhere.

- Joe Pacheco

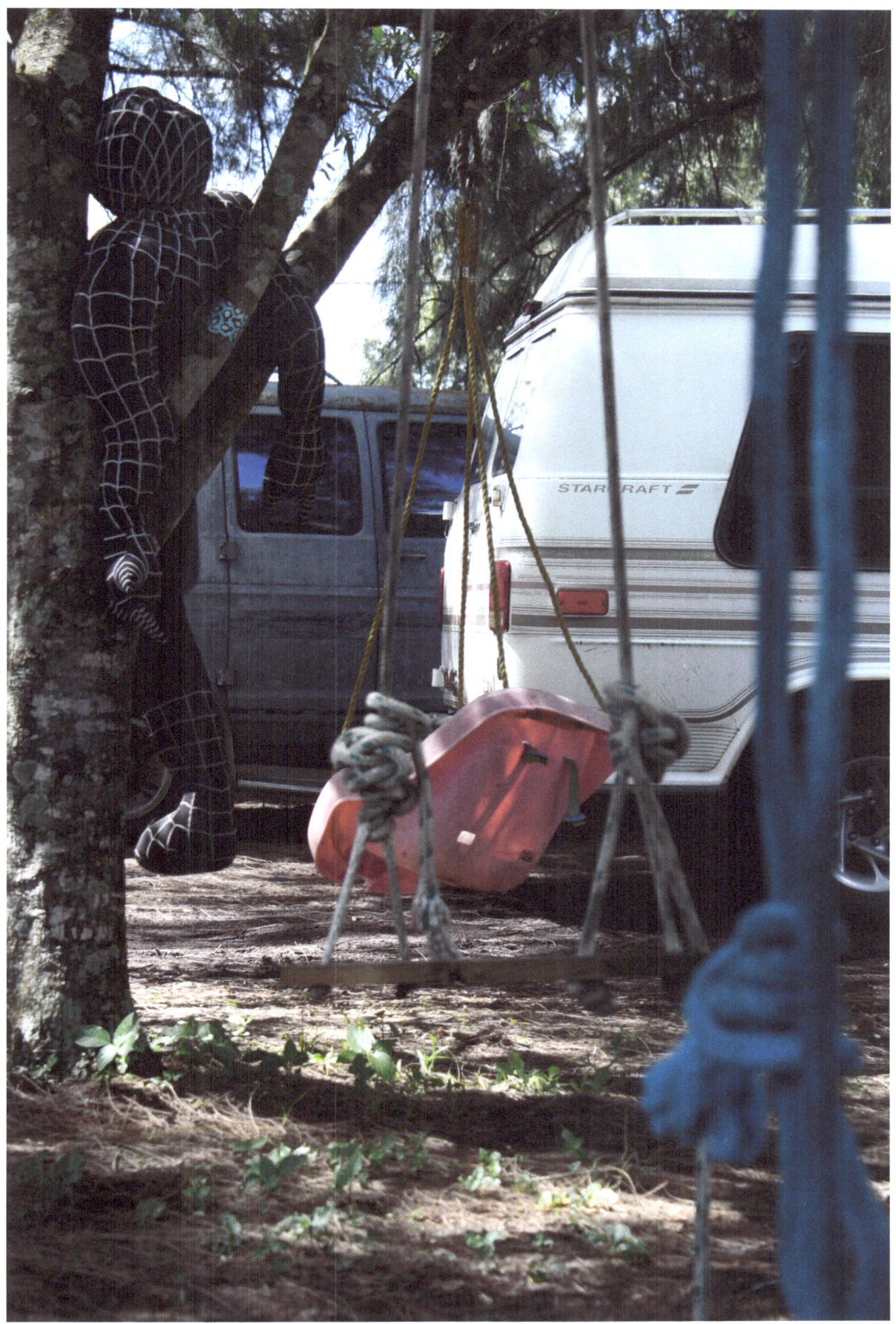

Off Prospect—*Beth Everhart*

Deport Yourself, It's Later Than You Think
Inspiration for Berry van Boekel's "Deport Yourself"

Deport yourself, it's later than you think,
Deport yourself, or you'll end up in the clink.
The year's gone by, economy's on the blink
Deport yourself, deport yourself, it's greater than you think.

You've worked at jobs no gringos want, you're always on the go,
To make enough for your family here and the one in Mexico,
But every time you settle down and think you've got it made,
You lose your latest job again to another Migra* raid.

Deport yourself, it's easier than you think,
Deport yourself, stop standing on the brink,
When you're back home, your life will be in synch,
Deport yourself, deport yourself, have a tequila drink.

You'll let our tomatoes go unpicked and rot upon the vine,
There won't be places cheap enough where we can sit and dine,
Our lawns and grounds will go ungroomed, our beds will be unmade,
But you'll be rich in your home town where no one's ever paid.

Deport yourself, your green card's long extinct,
Deport yourself, get back into the pink,
Your wife and kids will either swim or sink,
Deport yourself, deport yourself, it's greater than you think.

    Joe Pacheco

*Immigration authorities

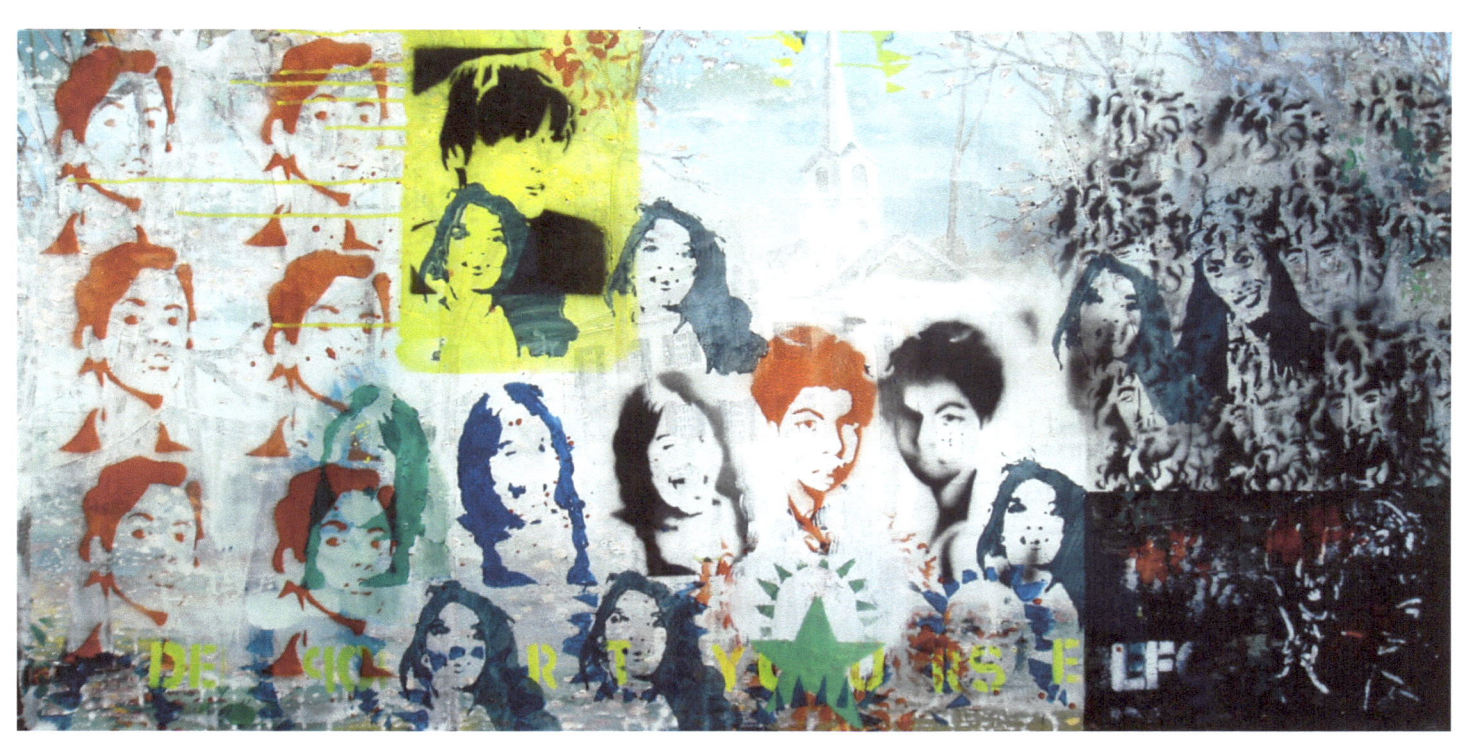

Deport Yourself—*Berry Van Boekel*

Tamiami Trail

Inspired by Scott Guelcher's "Tamiami Trail"

Big Biff got into his old Ford Taurus.
Dents told of history, bad parking places,
trees he didn't see, routine back up scrapes.

He starts a trip out to the Tamiami Trail on
this bright sunny day. No one knows where
it will take him down the smooth black tarmac.

Biff stops for gas at Wawa, knows the girl there,
buys sunflower seeds to spit shells out the window.
He wouldn't he caught dead at an Exxon-Mobil or Shell.

Biff goes off the main road, into a nature preserve.
Looks for a Flamingo, even a plastic one. None there,
He did see one Alligator, not sure it wasn't stuffed.
Angry, he runs over a Snake, and splatters two Frogs.
No sympathy, they needed to die. We all need to die. But
not her. Not her. Biff leans on the steering wheel and cries,

Yes, this trip is about death, and the cancerous road
that takes you to it. Fast food, lousy alcohol, cigarettes.
Stale relationships that grow empty and often violent on
both sides of this highway. Biff takes the exit off towards
the hospice. Cement cage where he sat by her bed, day after
day, until he heard the death rattle. But he wasn't done with her.
Friends say, move on, Buddy. Forget her. Get back to the golf course.
Biff wants to pick up a golf club and bang it on God's head. Why her?
He buys a pint of vodka, orders two McDonald double cheese burgers
with fries and heads North on the Tamiami Trail, in search of nothing.

When the last fry has been chewed, tears start again and won't stop.
Makes Biff floor the gas pedal. The Taurus almost lifts it's front wheels.
Faster, wilder, until he rams into an unmoving concrete bridge ramp. The
Taurus ricochets, spirals in the air, enters the water like Eleanor Powell,
ending upside down. The coral rips it open. Biff hangs by his seat belt,
and the empty McDonald's bag joins everything else red with his blood.

- Sidney B. Simon

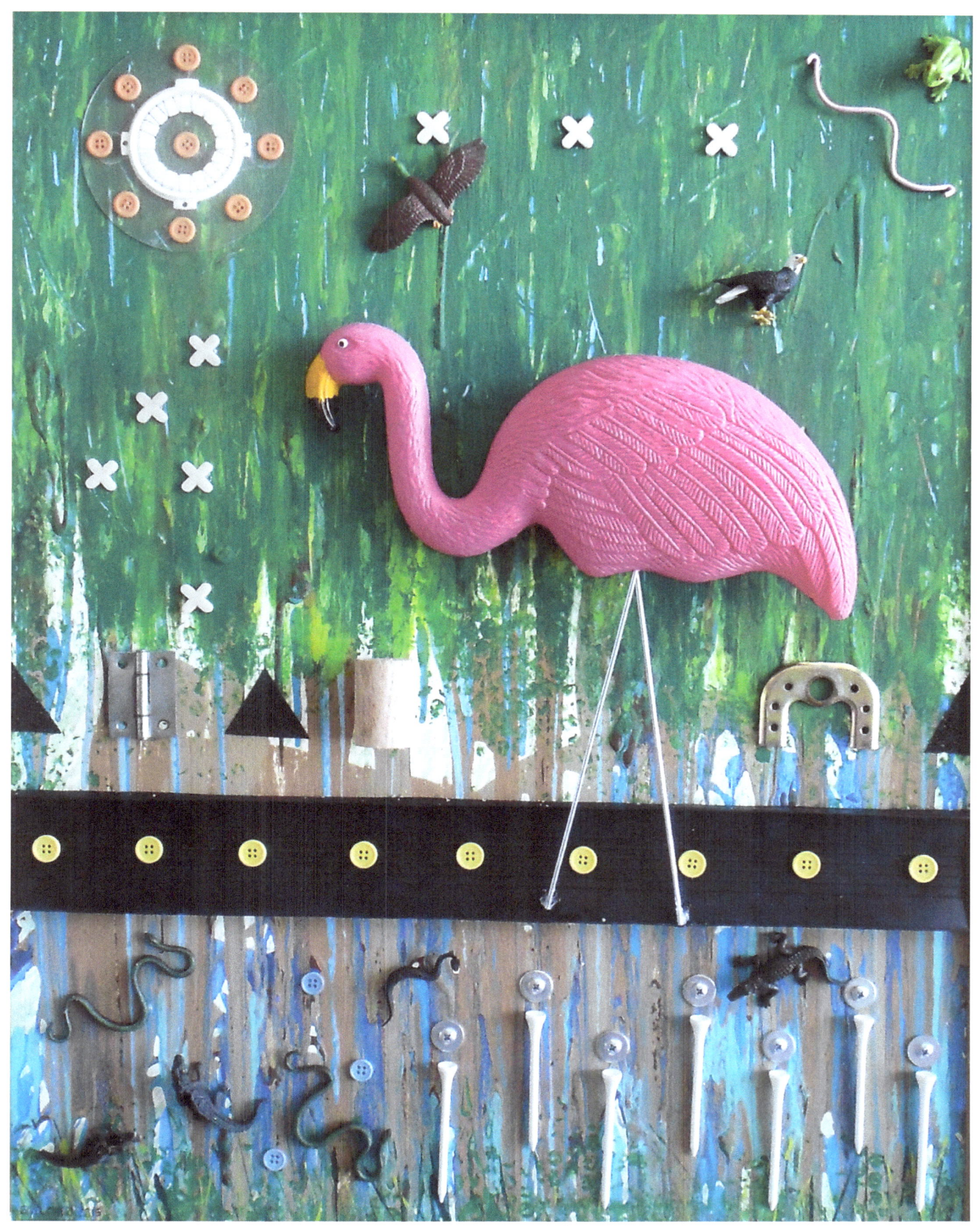

Tamiami Trail—*Scott Guelcher*

Simple Questions the Widow Asks Herself

Inspiration for artist Terry Lynn's "Kiss"

Will I be content to die without ever again being kissed? Can I be
happy to sleep for the rest of my life without the warmth of a body
near by, never again to be held close when nightmares tear me awake?

I'm free now. Is it truly joyful to no longer be pressed to think
about, or think for, any man in my life? And, what about dumb
little freedoms? Will I celebrate the freedom to plop around the
house all morning in a coffee-stained house coat, if I want to?

Or never having to sit at the movies in a row someone else prefers?
But, will I still miss bumping into a hand in the popcorn bag, sometimes
having salt kissed off my fingers?   Do I prefer riding home alone, no
one to argue with about a movie's rambling and bumbling plot?

But do I really, really love knowing dinner never has to be cooked?
That I can eat ice cream right out of the half-gallon box, having no
witnesses, taking no prisoners? You're free," I whisper to myself.
"You won't miss the melodrama a man wears like cheap after-shave."
Yet, am I someone with skin that has forgotten what touch brings?
Would I live just fine when my hands are in dish suds and there's no man
nearby who might come again to kiss the back of my neck before his
arms encircled my breasts and asked, "Honey, do you need any help?"

And here's another not so simple question. It comes up on lonely, gray
mornings with the sound of the wood pecker trying to chase the gloom
by tapping love calls on the neighbor's tin roof.   Will I live peacefully
with this freedom if only memory alone celebrates the familiar weight
of a man in hunger stretched out upon the length of my yearning body?
I know all too well that libidos grow limp, dry days pass, there are
distractions enough. But I am haunted because I was gifted, by fiery
memories. The simple question hangs like wisteria. Just this one question.
Will I choose to die without the kisses and all that comes with them?

- Sidney B. Simon

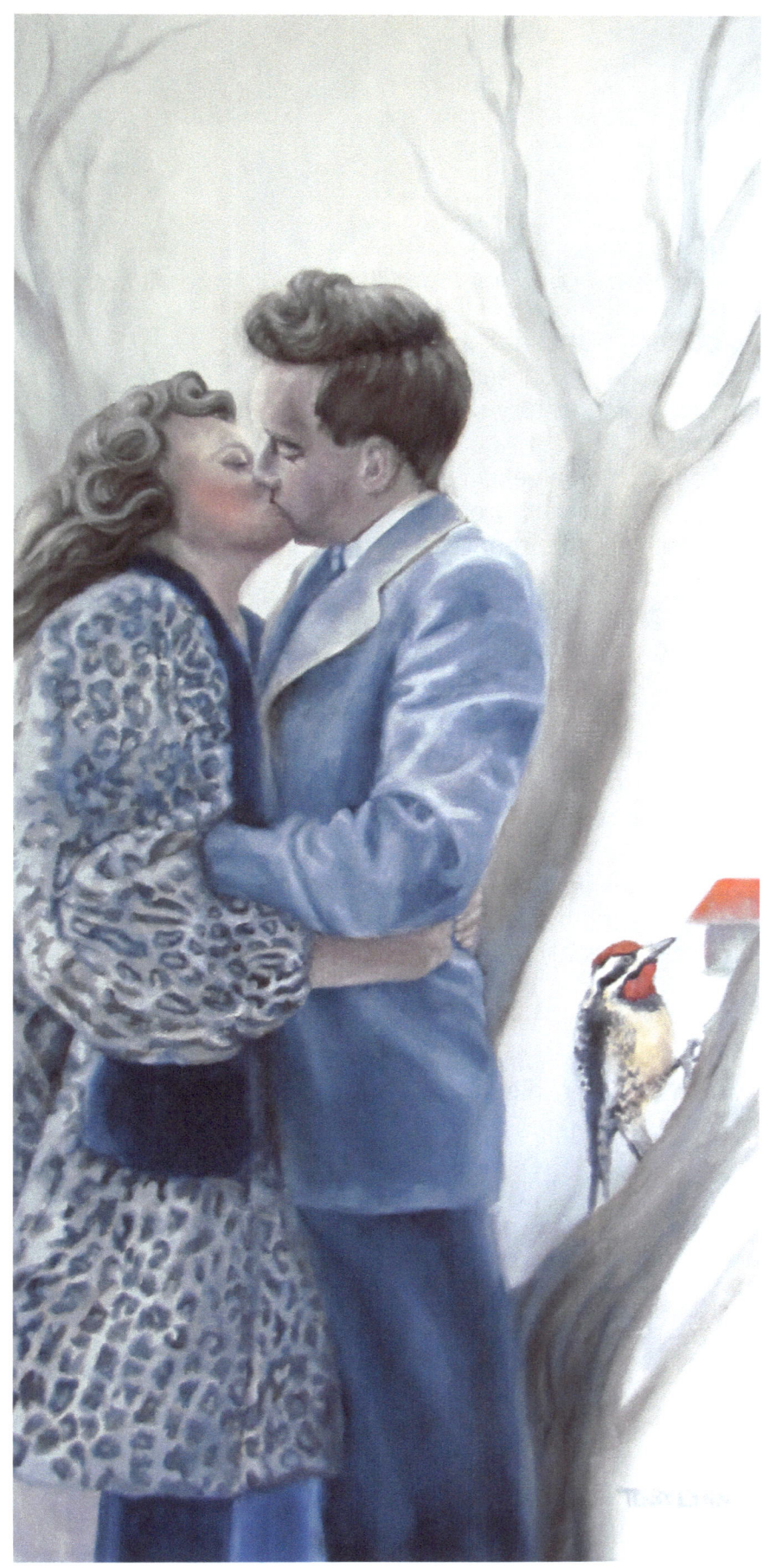

Kiss—*Terry Lynn*

Hey Carlos
Inspired by Paul David Adamick's "Carlos Sells Flowers and Fruit on the Beach"

Your head bursting with blossoms,
you are the first line in your family's story,
writing the continuing history of America.

You work the beach on weekends,
your Latin charm laden with tropical fruit
and flowers, selling to the touristas.

Sun-burdened, a hot sandy beach is no escape
from the fields of peppers and tomatoes
you pick all week. Ah Carlos...

Everyone knows you are not from here.
Have you noticed, people look right through
you, ignoring your callused hands, feet?

Carlos, you are drawing lines in sand, you are
willing to walk beyond borders, yet some
think you a threat, pedaling your pineapples.

No border, no boundary can contain your spirit.
Carlos, you are who we Americans once were,
we are who you will become.

-Lorraine Walker Williams

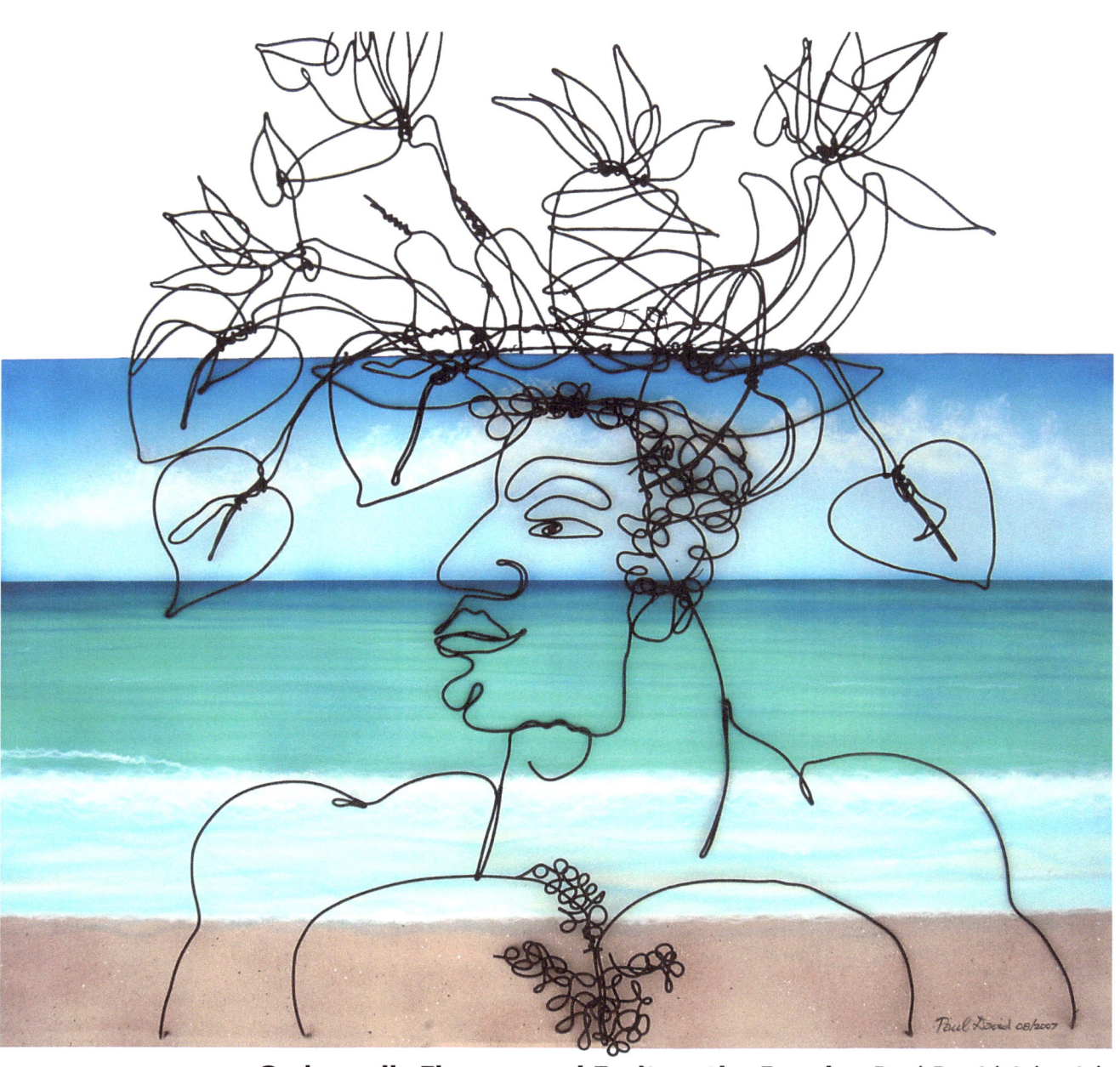

Carlos sells Flowers and Fruit on the Beach—*Paul David Adamick*

Roses

Inspiration for artist Dennis Church's "Flowers at a Farmer's Market"

If I could give you roses,
the scent of bloom in June,
I'd risk the prick of thorn
petaled in perfume.

If I could give you roses,
buds unfolding in sun's glaze,
I'd kneel on dampened earth
and gather summer days.

If I could give you roses,
cut fresh with morning dew,
I'd place them in a vase,
each pink and crimson hue.

Yet seasons change
and petals lose their place.
So I will give you roses,
in lines that words can trace.

You can hold them in your hand,
taste and touch their bloom.
These are roses that will last
beyond the bonds of June.

-Lorraine Walker Williams

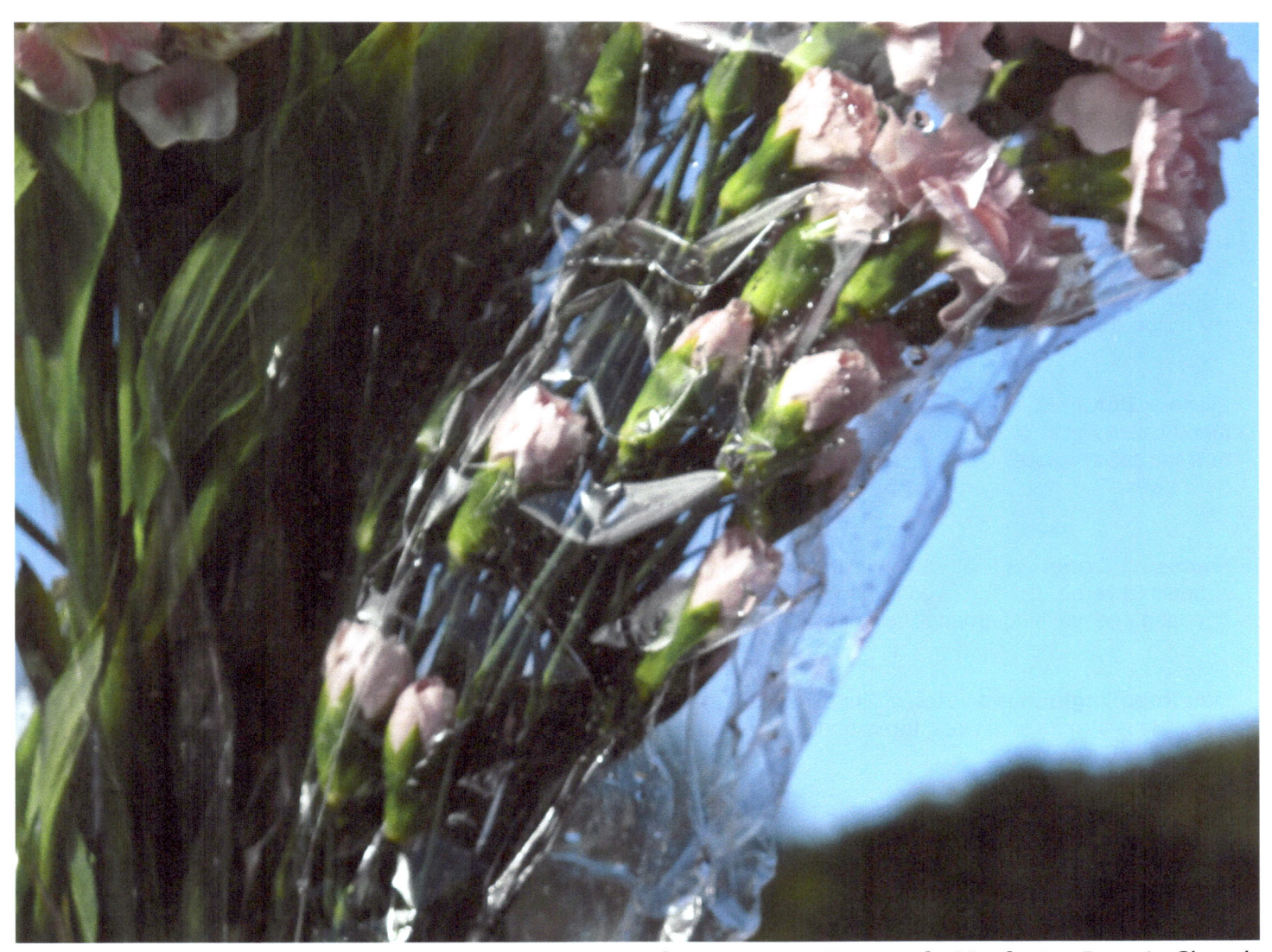

Flowers at a Farmer's Market—*Dennis Church*

Artists and Poets Information

Paul David Adamick: A retired elementary art teacher of 41 years, I teach art classes at Cape Coral Art Studio where I teach "Drawing with Wire" and "Draw To Paint" for novice artists. I also do raku clay masks with fused glass headdresses.

Maria Bouloux Hochschild has spent most of her life living in different parts of the world. British born, she came to live in the US nine years ago and lives part time in Florida. Now retired, she spends much of her time painting portraits. She paints from her own photographs and always searches for faces that draw a particular emotion.

Dennis Church shows his photographs nationally and internationally. Locally, his next showing will feature his photographs at DAAS Coop Gallery in Ft Myers, in April 2017. This fall two of his photographs will appear in a book: *Bystander: A History of Street Photography*.

Honey Costa. My spirited watercolors and collages are reflections of my personal interests in life. I live in a world of color thru the inspirational ambiance and beauty of the tropical vistas and people of the Caribbean and Florida. It is my joy to capture these colors of our tropical paradise and create pleasure for my viewers. Art is my raison d'etre.

Eleanor Dominek is a portrait and landscape painter working in oil and pastel. She has exhibited in national juried shows, including the Pastel Society of America's Annual Exhibition. "As an artist I feel an urgency to capture the sacred space. The process of painting the landscape —its light, shadow, and color – brings me balance. I am awake".

Marissa J. Douglass is a newcomer to the ArtPoems group. She enjoys studying people, metaphysics, baking, antiquated vernacular and bygone slang. She is currently finishing her bachelors in English at FGCU, with hopes of eating and teaching around the world. She loves poetry and her dog.

Dan Reed England is a licensed clinical social worker, working in the mental health field, and is originally from Iowa. He is also an avid wood turner, builds furniture, and enjoys kayaking.

Beth Everhart is a visual artist, working predominantly in the medium of photography. Her most recent exhibits in Fort Myers include a found snapshot exhibition at Arts for ACT entitled *A Small Vacation*, the Juror's Choice Award in the 28th Annual All Florida Juried Exhibit at Lee County Alliance for the Arts, and participation in the *Fort Myers Founding Females Exhibition*. Beth received her Master of Fine Arts degree in 1989 from Hunter College, and currently teaches Fine Arts at Fort Myers High School.

Former English teacher, **Joyce Berrian Ferrari** resides with her husband in Fort Myers and in Lavalette, NJ. Joyce is enjoying her third year as a poet-participant in ArtPoems. Many of her poems evolve from her life experiences and her observations of nature.

Chris Godwin loves the power of story, the word, and the visual. A published author, retired college administrator and Professor Emerita of English (State University of NY-SUNY Orange), she thrives each winter in Sanibel's rich creative sun, sand and shells.

Sandy Greco finds inspiration in personal experience. A retired physician, she attended the University of Chicago, and resided in NJ before moving to Sanibel.

Scott Guelcher's style has become well known in Southwest Florida. His blend of Pop Art Images and abstract backgrounds has attracted galleries to feature his artwork. A graduate of FGCU in 2005, he teaches art at Island Coast H.S. and was commissioned to make two Azul statues for the FGCU campus.

Linda Lally is currently a Tai Chi instructor, and artist. She is a former elementary teacher from Santa Fe, New Mexico, where art was the core of her curriculum. She attended Art Students League in NYC, Lincoln College Oxford , graduated from Cornell University. Her art is inspired by years of world travel and living in beautiful places.

Terry Lynn's paintings have been exhibited in national and local juried art exhibitions. She had won honorable mention in abstract division in The Artist Magazine 2013. In addition, her work can be found in private collections across the country.

Mary Beth Lundgren belongs to SWFL Poets. She's authored two poetic picture books plus a teen novel, along with many short pieces, including Broadsides, for kids and adults. Born in Ohio, she moved to Florida with her husband in 1999.

Doug MacGregor is a native of Binghamton, N.Y., a graduate of Syracuse University and has lived in Southwest Florida since 1988. Doug enjoys drawing editorial cartoons, writing and illustrating children's books, and playing harmonica in local bands. He is currently Coordinator for the Arts in Healthcare program, bringing the expressive arts to patients and families within Lee Health.

Gary McLouth, award-winning fiction writer and published poet, teaches composition and American literature at Florida SouthWestern State College in Fort Myers Florida. He has been an Art Poems' poet since 2013 and serves as EMCEE for the 2017 edition of the Art Poems Program.

Joe Pacheco is Co-Chair of ArtPoems. *Sanibel Joe's Songbook* was published in 2013. Named Literary Artist of the Year in 2008 by the Alliance for the Arts, he has performed his poetry in N.Y.C. and Miami, and writes a poetry column for the *Sanibel Islander*.

Roy Rodriguez. As a photographer, I attract impressions of the world around me. They have a certain hidden beauty which I discover and then using craftsmanship I charm my audience to look closely.   I say, "look at my world, look at what I see, let's appreciate how much beauty and mystery there is in everything around us".

Sidney B. Simon is the author of a dozen books, mostly on Values Clarification. *CHEAP GRAMPA IN ACTION* is his most recent. He's a Theater Critic and MC for "Stories for Grownups." Sid was Literary Artist of the Year, 2011, almost as happy an event as being in Art Poems right from the very first year.

Lorraine Walker Williams. Creator and Chair Emeritus of ArtPoems was nominated for the Pushcart Prize twice. *Simply Sanibel Poems* is her fifth book of poetry. Literary Artist of the Year 2009, she writes a weekly poetry column for *Santivachronicle.com*   lorrainewalkerwilliams.com

Hailing from the Netherlands **Berry van Boekel** has exhibited with the prestigious alternative non-profit space White Columns in New York; Country Club Projects in Cincinnati, Peel Gallery in Houston, at the NADA Art Fair in Miami. He received an MFA from The Ohio State University. He currently teaches art at Florida SouthWestern State College and at the Center For the Arts at Bonita Springs.